SHORT CUTS

INTRODUCTIONS TO FILM STUDIES

DOCUMENTARY

THE MARGINS OF REALITY

PAUL WARD

WALLFLOWER

LONDON and NEW YORK

A Wallflower Paperback

First published in Great Britain in 2005 by
Wallflower Press
6a Middleton Place, Langham Street, London W1W 7TE
www.wallflowerpress.co.uk

A catalogue record for this book is available from the British Library

ISBN 1 904764 59 2

Book design by Rob Bowden Design

Printed in Great Britain by Antony Rowe Ltd, Chippenham, Wiltshire

CONTENTS

ACKNOWLEDGEMENTS

I would like to thank Mike Wayne and Brian Winston for reading and commenting on earlier drafts of the manuscript. I also wish to thank the following for their help with images: Andy Glynne of the Documentary Filmmakers Group (http://www.dfglondon.com) for the image from *Obsessively Compulsive*; Marc Isaacs for the image from *Lift*; Artangel for the image from *The Battle of Orgreave*; Bob Sabiston for the image from *Snack and Drink*. All other images courtesy of the British Film Institute.

INTRODUCTION

This book aims to give a brief introduction to and overview of some of the key features, moments and theoretical debates of its subject matter – documentary. There has been an enormous expansion in scholarship relating to documentary in recent years; this book cannot do justice to the breadth and depth of all the issues relating to this area. The aim of this introduction is to re-evaluate some of what can be seen as the key problems with actually defining documentary in the first place. This will mean thinking through the distinction between fiction and nonfiction, and where documentary might lie in relation to other forms of factual film and media. It will therefore mean looking at a broader range of material than is commonly supposed to come under the heading 'documentary'. Some of what is discussed here would usually be categorised as 'drama documentary', other material borrows heavily from the conventions of investigative journalism. The main point to understand from the outset is that there is a large range of modes of factual film and television and 'documentary' is often used as an umbrella term to describe them all. As we shall see, 'documentary' originally meant a very specific kind of factual film, and it has now become problematic to use it as a catch-all term. This problem has partly been addressed by the various attempts to devise descriptive modes of documentary (see chapter one) – sub-categories that make clear that different documentaries will do different things. It is equally clear, however, that factual films and programmes have now reached such a level of hybridity, that it is very difficult to sustain a notion of there being stable categories.

With all this in mind, chapter one offers an overview of some of the dilemmas facing anyone who attempts to discuss documentary as a form.

The main point is that those engaged in documentary-related activity range across a wide spectrum of 'communities of practice' and it is the discussion and debate between them that means that the form is constantly in flux. We shall also explore the vital role that the spectator plays in understanding, and 'placing' documentary, and how people negotiate the often very complex shifting sands that constitute documentary production and reception.

Chapter two moves on to examine the notion of drama-documentary and the relationship between fiction and nonfiction through a study of some recent television films that use real people (or real people's testimony) as the basis for a re-enacted, improvised drama. In most of these cases, what we are watching is not straightforwardly 'documentary', but it is certainly not simply fiction either. The second part of the chapter looks at the different ways in which the story of Aileen Wuornos, the woman who murdered seven men and was executed in 2002, has been told. A comparative analysis of the different versions of the 'same' story will draw out some of the ways that documentary modality, as well as versions of 'the truth', can be shaped in the name of dramatic license.

Chapter three continues to delineate specific arguments about (re)construction and (re)enactment that have been touched upon so far. The focus in this chapter is the *historical* dimension of certain documentary modes. The films examined offer a glimpse of a 'hidden' or obscured history and how particular types of dramatised documentary material can help us to revive neglected (or suppressed) historical events. If the role of documentary is to assert things about the world we inhabit (and this includes the world of the historical past), then such films have a vitally important part to play, in the ways that they draw out and amplify some of the underlying tensions and sensibilities of the times they depict.

Chapters four and five move on to examine two relatively under-explored areas within 'documentary studies': comedy and animation. Chapter four's overview of documentary and comedy is not only interested in those texts that satirise or parody documentary forms, though it does look at certain tendencies such as mock-documentaries, spoofs and so on. The chapter is also interested in examining what happens when the (apparently 'opposed') modalities of documentary and comedy meet. The former is associated with seriousness, sobriety and making truth claims or assertions about the real world. Comedy is commonly (and mistakenly) seen as a mode that is somehow incompatible with these apparently 'lofty' aims.

Chapter five offers a much-needed look at documentary and animation. Animation has long been associated with subjectivity, interiority and an inherent 'manipulation' or 'constructedness' that documentary appears to eschew. And yet, as argued throughout the book, documentaries are also constructed. The overarching argument is not that we should look at these types of documentary production and think of them as 'marginal', but that we should move beyond simplistic notions of what is 'central' and 'marginal' in the first place. 'Documentary' in the twenty-first century is a complex set of overlapping discourses and practices, and we need our theories, critical approaches and – perhaps most of all – our documentarists to be equipped to recognise and deal with this fact.

As the chapter outlines above make clear, this book is not intended as a simple 'introduction' to documentary. The choice instead has been to concentrate on what are held to be some of the key issues and ways into understanding this diverse field. Some readers may find these choices somewhat idiosyncratic, but it is important not to simply offer a potted history of the field but rather raise some questions about how we define and discuss that field. In this respect, the notion of 'margins' flagged up in the title of this book is less a call for us to pay attention to under-investigated areas just for the sake of it and more a recognition of the dynamic ways in which all forms of nonfiction media are developing.

One of the key and abiding (in terms of continuing influence) engagements with documentary as a form was provided by John Grierson, something discussed in more detail in chapter one. He is credited with the first English-language use of the term 'documentary', when he stated (in a review of Robert Flaherty's *Moana* (1926, US)) that the film had 'documentary value' (Grierson 1979: 25).[1] He was also the driving force behind the British documentary movement of the 1930s, where state-sponsored films were made under the aegis of the Crown Film Unit, the Empire Marketing Board and the GPO Film Unit. Many of the films produced in this era went on to have a profound influence on the documentary form, and rehearsed many of the theoretical and critical issues (relating to use of reconstruction, 'creative' use of sound and image) that are still debated today. *Coalface* (Alberto Cavalcanti, 1935, UK), for example, is a strange combination of dour, expository voiceover, maps and expressionistic visuals with experimental sound. Grierson was critical of Dziga Vertov's experimental paean to Soviet Moscow, *Man with a Movie Camera* (1929, USSR), dismissing it as 'a snapshot album … [that] just dithers about on the surface of life' (1966: 127), but some of the British films with which Grierson was associated showed clear signs of a similar interest in the experimental potential of documentary filmmaking.

Arguably even more influential were the various documentary filmmakers who emerged after the Second World War, who forged an 'observational' aesthetic very different from the obviously creative interpretations of Grierson or Vertov. US-based filmmakers such as Richard Leacock, Robert Drew and the Maysles Brothers were committed to a form of documentary that appeared to merely observe the events that unfolded before the camera, and they were helped immeasurably in this by the emergence of portable cameras and sound recording equipment. Some of the contradictions in so-called 'direct cinema' are returned to in chapter one, but it is certainly the case that this form of documentary, with its fly-on-the-wall pretensions, has had an enormous impact upon a wide range of factual television formats; indeed, it is not too much of an exaggeration to say that the vast majority of documentary and factual programming on television bears its influence in one way or another. From the immediacy of broadcast news reportage to day-in-the-life docu-soaps to other reality TV formats such as *Big Brother* or *Wife Swap*, there is a foundation of observed events or behaviour that owes something to direct cinema. That all of these examples do very different things with the 'observed' material they use – and they are 'read' in very different ways by their respective audiences – is testament to the hybridity and diversity of the contemporary factual/documentary field.

Although the institutional role of television in shaping this variety of factual formats will be discussed to some extent, we shall not spend too much time discussing 'reality TV' *per se*. There are a number of recent excellent studies that cover this ground (see, for example Kilborn 2003; Holmes and Jermyn 2004; Biressi and Nunn 2005; Hill 2005). Many of these concentrate on programmes like *Big Brother* and other hybrids that use elements of the game show and the fly-on-the-wall/surveillance documentary. Along with the docu-soap, the other main innovation in recent factual television output, such programming exhibits a decisive turn towards packaging the documentary/factual format in a way that is irrefutably populist, with an eye on entertainment (and ratings) rather than the more educative role envisioned for it by people such as Grierson. The deregulation of British television, along with the emergence of new satellite/digital technology, has led to a plethora of channels – and the wide range of reality programmes have been used to fill this vast amount of airtime. Here the discussion is limited (in chapters two and three) to those documentary-inflected programmes and films that attempt to offer a more interesting and challenging use of real people and their lives than is often the case with the bulk of reality TV programming.

If there is a central strand running through this book it is that which arguably characterises many of the debates about documentary. That is, the tension between, on the one hand, the capturing of some aspect of the real world and the people who inhabit it, and on the other hand the inevitable use of aesthetic and representational devices to achieve that aim. Also, the notion of performance has become increasingly central to debates about how documentary and factual programming function and address their audience. As we shall see in subsequent chapters, the way in which subjects of documentary (or pseudo-documentary, such as the various kinds of drama-documentary) behave in ways that can at least be recognised (and often condemned) as 'performing for the cameras' has taken documentary makers and viewers into a hugely interesting area. The notion of actively shaping or interpreting one's material, and the issue of performance, have always been factors for documentarists, though it is certainly true that they are now more recognised and reflected upon as issues than was previously the case. All factual/documentary films and programmes need to be thought about in the light of these important issues. As we move into the twenty-first century, and this field becomes even more diverse and complex, the hope is that some of the issues discussed in this book will be of use to those with an interest in documentary of all kinds.

1   DEFINING DOCUMENTARY

What is a documentary?

We shall begin by looking at the central tension that constitutes all debates about documentary: the relationship between reality and artifice. John Grierson's famous dictum, 'the creative interpretation of actuality', was one of the first encapsulations of this tension, and has been quoted, misquoted and rephrased many times over the years. John Corner refers to the 'art of record' (1996); Brian Winston sums it up as 'claiming the real' (1995). In all of these attempts to adequately capture the meaning of documentary, there is the same dilemma: how to deal with and understand something that quite clearly is attempting to represent *reality* (or some part of reality), but as it does so, uses specific *aesthetic* devices. A commonsense suggestion is that the aesthetics somehow *distort* or *change* the reality being represented. This central issue has troubled documentary filmmakers and theorists (the latter more than the former, it has to be said) and has arguably had a debilitating effect on understanding documentaries.

Secondly, questions of documentary history and the development of the form will be examined. The tendency towards a 'canonical' understanding of documentary, and what Stella Bruzzi (2000) has pointed out is an overly 'genealogical' notion of its development, are things that have (again) held back our understanding. Elsewhere in the book we shall consider types of documentary work that might be deemed to be 'marginal', but the suggestion here is that we need a more complex typology of modes of documentary, and how they interact, if we are to fully grasp the depth and breadth of the field. In this sense, the material focused upon in the rest of the book should be seen as where new and dynamic understandings of the term documentary reside, as different modes will change how we understand the term. It is one of the overarching aims of this book to not merely champion the 'marginal' and make a case for certain 'neglected' films, but rather to shift the emphasis onto viewing all documentary practice in a wider context. As we shall see, the notions of 'marginal' and 'central' are subject to change and re-definition, depending on context and usage.

So, what is a 'documentary'? A good starting point is to examine the relationship between the categories 'nonfiction' and 'documentary'. As we shall see, these terms are intimately related (and sometimes used interchangeably) and anyone looking to understand what 'documentary' might mean needs to think about the category 'nonfiction'. (Clearly, this also suggests that we need to think about the relationship to 'fiction' as a category – this is something looked at in some detail in chapter two). A nonfiction film or programme is one in which the people and events depicted are known to have (or are asserted to have) a real-world existence. Unlike the fictional mode, where places and characters may be completely fabricated, the nonfictional is a realm where there is a basis in the world of actuality. This seems straightforward enough – fiction is 'made up', nonfiction is 'real' – and yet there are countless nuances and points on a spectrum that suggest that this relationship is more fraught than it first appears.

All documentary films are nonfictional, but not all nonfiction films are documentaries. Added to this is the complication of what happens when films that are agreed to be documentaries use techniques and conventions more readily associated with *fictional* storytelling. As we shall see, there is nothing inherently 'fictional' about narrative structure and the editing styles that have developed to tell stories. The key distinction is never one of form or style, but rather of purpose and context. As mock-documentaries prove, we can have fictional, completely fabricated films that mimic the textures and ebb and flow of certain types of documentary. Likewise, there are documentary films that use dramatic structure, reconstructions and the like in order to add to their impact. And there are fictional films that use a certain shooting style and dialogue which evokes 'documentariness' in order to bolster their claims to authenticity.

At its most basic, a nonfictional film might involve the simple recording of an event. The early *actualities* of the Lumière Brothers – trains arriving, workers leaving – are of course nonfictional. The Zapruder footage of the assassination of JFK is nonfictional. The video footage of Rodney King being beaten, shot by George Holliday, is nonfictional. These films have a clear indexical link to a profilmic world – a world that 'happens' irrespective of whether or not the camera is present – and they appear to simply 'show' or record the events they depict. One of the reasons the Zapruder and Holliday films have had such impact is precisely because they capture, seemingly unawares, momentous events. Their status as images stems from their 'unstaged' basis. The Lumière films are slightly different in the sense that they do show some signs of rudimentary staging. As the workers leave the factory, we sense that they just perhaps are 'performing' this exit for the benefit of the camera. Does this matter?

This notion of 'staging' material, to then film it *as if* it happened there and then, unprompted, in front of the camera – basically, to present the staged as if it were unstaged – is one of the great red herrings of documentary. A common assumption appears to be that if any staging of any kind has taken place that this somehow invalidates the documentary status of what we are looking at. The hugely influential US 'direct cinema' practitioners, for example, made it one of their 'rules' to never stage anything for the cameras – they had a belief that truth could only be represented via the literal unfolding of events, captured as if the camera and crew were not present.

However, the contention here is that staging is an unavoidable part of the filmmaking process – as unavoidable as pointing the camera at something, editing, using sound[1] – and it is not staging (or dramatic (re)construction) *per se* that is the problem, but our attitudes towards it. These attitudes are often based on an untenable essentialist notion of what documentary 'is' and bizarrely seem to see documentary as an apparently unchanging mode of filmmaking. The only unchanging thing about documentary is that it is a form that makes assertions or truth claims about the real world or real people in that world (including the real world of history); *how* it does this *is* something that is subject to change. In this respect, films and programmes as diverse as *Man with a Movie Camera*, *Coalface*, *The War Game* (Peter Watkins, 1965, UK), *Salesman* (Albert and David Maysles and Charlotte Zwerin, 1969, US), *Sans Soleil* (Chris Marker, 1982, Fr.), *The Battle of Orgreave* (Mike Figgis, 2001, UK) and the *Animated Minds* (Andy Glynne, 2003, UK) series of films can all arguably be termed documentaries. They all use very different techniques and styles, and represent very different aspects of the world. Even with *The War Game*, which represents a possible *future* world, the intention is clearly that of a documentary (like Watkins' *Culloden* (1964, UK) from the previous year, which reconstructed a historical past). The *Animated Minds* films use animation, and therefore do not have that indexical visual link with the actuality they depict. Nevertheless, the techniques used are with a view to assert something about a real actual person: the result is therefore a form of 'documentary'. We shall return to some of these examples in more detail in subsequent chapters, particularly this notion of staging and reconstructing, and how it impacts on the 'documentary status' of certain films. For the moment let us concentrate on some of the basic positions on documentary as a form.

Although John Grierson was not really the very first person to coin the phrase 'documentary', and there have been some disputes over his status as the 'father' of the documentary movement (see, for example, Pronay 1989), it is certainly the case that his interventions and pronouncements on the subject have been hugely influential. Grierson had no problem with the use of the 'dramatic' in the 'documentary' context. Indeed, it was the injection of 'drama', an underlying dramatic organising principle, that distinguished documentary films proper from what Grierson called the 'lower categories' of nonfiction film such as newsreel or lecture films (1966: 145). Though the latter also had as their basis 'natural material', what they lacked was the *organisation* that defined documentary. As Grierson says about the so-called 'lecture films':

> They do not dramatise, they do not even dramatise an episode: they describe, and even expose, but in any aesthetic sense, only rarely reveal. Herein is their formal limit, and it is unlikely that they will make any considerable contribution to the fuller art of the documentary. (1966: 146)

The distinction that Grierson draws here is one that we can still arguably see in the bifurcation between what is understood as 'documentary proper' and 'investigative journalism', now almost exclusively the preserve of broadcasters. As Grierson puts it, once one moves beyond the lower categories, 'we pass from the plain (or fancy) descriptions of natural material, to arrangements, rearrangements and creative shapings of it' (ibid.).

Here we almost have the now-famous dictum 'the creative interpretation of actuality'.[2] The important thing here is that Grierson makes no bones about using creative 'shaping' – indeed, this is what defines and distinguishes documentary proper. This flies in the face of the still-prevailing orthodoxy in the wake of direct cinema: that documentary should not only consist of 'natural material', but that this should appear to viewers as objectively, transparently and 'undoctored' as possible.

These notions of objectivity and transparency resonate through the history of documentary and other forms of nonfictional/factual programming. Certainly with regard to television documentary output, with its strong links to broadcast journalism and current affairs, there seems to be a distrust of anything that deviates from a 'fair and balanced' position. As we shall see in chapter three, this position is problematic to say the least, but has everything to do with the dominance of one specific kind of documentary practice (direct cinema and its variants), combined with the foregrounding of professional journalistic techniques and conventions, where 'balance' and 'impartiality' are key elements.

The problem was – and still is – that there is a perceived problem in balancing what appears to be diametrically opposed tendencies: the capturing of natural material on the one hand, and the creative shaping or interpretation of it on the other. As Brian Winston puts it: 'The supposition that any "actuality" is left after "creative treatment" can now be seen as being at best naïve and at worst a mark of duplicity' (1995: 11). The problem with such a position is, as Stella Bruzzi points out, that it renders virtually impossible any form of documentary. The assumption seems to be that a proper documentary aims to render actuality purely, accurately and objectively, and that the imposition of any 'creative treatment' inevitably gets in the way of this project. However, this is not the aim of documentary, and nor should it be. As Bruzzi puts it, much documentary criticism and theory seems based on a 'simple but erroneous' claim, 'that the minute an individual becomes involved in the representation of reality, the integrity of that reality is irretrievably lost' (2000: 4). Of course there are issues to be debated here – to do with the nature and extent of use of reconstruction and re-enactment, the types of intervention or 'treatment' that different filmmakers use, the role of actual people in (semi-)dramatised situations, and so on – but we have to begin by agreeing that it *is* possible for documentary to be *both* a recording *and* a treatment. Bruzzi therefore appears correct when she notes that documentary, if it is anything, is a 'perpetual negotiation between the real event and its representation ... the two remain distinct but interactive' (2000: 9). As the term 'negotiation' suggests, the roles of the documentarists and the spectators are a crucial part of this process of understanding, so the discourses surrounding documentary – the different ways in which they are understood and categorised – are also crucial.

Rather than seeing documentaries, as a general category, as an inevitably failed attempt to render experience or certain situations *directly*, we should therefore recognise that the aesthetic choices made are merely the formal dimension and have no necessary say in whether or not something is a 'documentary'. What makes a documentary a documentary resides somewhere else, in the complex interaction between text, context, producer and spectator. As Noël Carroll puts it, in objecting to what he sees as a misguided focus by some critics and theorists on a formal distinction between fiction and nonfiction:

> The distinction between nonfiction film and fiction film cannot be grounded in differences of formal technique, because, when it comes to technique, fiction and nonfiction filmmakers can and do imitate each other ... The distinction between nonfiction and fiction, therefore, does not collapse with the recognition of stylistic correlations, since the distinction never rested upon such formal or technical differentiae in the first place. (1996: 286–7)

In other words, one cannot point to so-called 'fictional' devices (narrative trajectory, cross-cutting) in a documentary and state that these devices, in and of themselves, invalidate that film's documentary status. Likewise, one cannot point to handheld camerawork or certain types of voiceover in a fiction film and state that these devices alter the film's fictional status. This is not to say that the use and abuse of specific conventions and, indeed, *how* such conventions come to be associated with certain types of filmmaking (and levels of ability to make meaningful statements about the real world) is not a fascinating and useful question to ask. In many respects these issues are what this book sets out to deal with. But it needs emphasising that the use of certain conventions and techniques is not the basis of a text's status vis-à-vis the real world. If it were, then *The Office*

(BBC, series one – 2001; series two – 2003, UK) would *be* a documentary; *The Thin Blue Line* (Errol Morris, 1988, US) would *be* a fiction film. This is clearly not the case, so their status as documentary or fiction must stem from something else. If we compare *The Office* to *Someone to Watch Over Me* (BBC, 2004, UK), a docu-soap about social services in Bristol, there are clear similarities in terms of form. The open-ended, ongoing, narrative; the emphasis on workplace; a similar shooting style. *Someone to Watch Over Me* uses voiceover narration at certain points, whilst *The Office* does not, and one can occasionally hear an off-camera question in the social services docu-soap, asking one of the characters for clarification. *The Office*, on the other hand, uses the convention of the straight-to-camera individual interview. The fact is, though, that despite the clear similarities in style and form, one of these programmes is recognised (or 'indexed', a term returned to below) as a fiction (albeit a fictional rendering of a recognisably docu-soap-like world: a mock-docu-soap or parody), whilst the other is recognised as a documentary.

One of the apparent problems is that it is difficult to come up with a generalisable set of criteria that *all* documentaries exhibit. If a film or programme uses certain techniques (reconstruction for example) it is accused of 'fictionalising' the material. Yet, as Carroll says, 'the distinction between nonfiction and fiction is a distinction between the commitments of the texts, not between the surface structures of the texts' (1996: 287). One of the problems of much so-called Grand Theory is that it attempts to 'explain' how things like film spectatorship 'work' in a way that flattens out and disavows any potential and useful differences between individual spectators, or the social groups to which they belong (see Austin 2005a). One simply cannot come up with a model of documentary that explains *all* documentary texts and their variants, precisely because it is an 'open concept' with 'fuzzy' boundaries. However, the work of classifying and cat-egorising should not be abandoned because of this. First of all, the existing categories, though far from perfect, do point to certain key similarities and enable us to talk about how documentaries work. Also, the existing categories bring to bear a *material* force on documentary practice in the sense that practitioners and audiences understand (or misunderstand) any documentary they watch by referring to categories of documentary. If a student is trying to explain what kind of documentary they are going to make, then they might use terms such as 'observational', 'fly-on-the-wall',

'Broomfield-esque' or 'mock-documentary'. We may have slightly different ideas of what these terms mean, but it is only by referring to them as a starting point that we can have any meaningful dialogue, and there is, in any case, a *general* consensus about what terms like this might mean. Furthermore, it is in the dialectical progression and hybridising of these categories – where a purely observational style meets a more interview-heavy, reflexive style for instance – that innovations are made. Thinking about how we understand and classify such a wide range of material is therefore of vital importance and should continue to remain central to any ongoing documentary studies project.

Modes and typologies: why categorise?

Bill Nichols has proposed a number of documentary modes and these typologies are extremely useful as a starting point in the spirit noted above. In *Representing Reality* (1991) he outlines a typology of: expository, observational, interactive and reflexive modes. More recently, in *Blurred Boundaries* (1994) Nichols expanded the typology to include what he terms the 'performative' mode of documentary. More recently still, in his *Introduction to Documentary* (2001) the notion of the 'interactive' mode appears to have been replaced by the term 'participatory' to cover much of the same sorts of documentary (though 'participatory' is a broader category, so perhaps it is more accurate to say that the participatory has subsumed the interactive). In both of these later works, there is also more recognition of what is termed the 'poetic' mode in documentary.

Expository documentaries are deemed to be those that address the spectator in a more or less direct manner, using supposedly 'didactic' conventions such as 'voice of God' narration on the soundtrack. A number – though by no means all – of the Griersonian documentaries made in the UK in the 1930s and 1940s might be termed expository in that they set out to tell the audience *about* something, 'how it is'. For Nichols, the strength of the expository mode is also its main weakness: it is too didactic, too sure of itself, and (in some discourses) too privileging of a certain way of looking at the world.

Conversely, observational documentary practice favours an aesthetic that aims for (apparent) neutrality – the proverbial 'fly-on-the-wall' that merely looks on and does not in any way interfere, intervene or (again, supposedly) creatively shape the material that unfolds. Direct cinema practitioners such as Robert Drew, Richard Leacock, D. A. Pennebaker, and the Maysles Brothers, as well as Fred Wiseman (who has made many films about American institutions, such as *High School* (1968, US) and *Hospital* (1970, US)) are all observational filmmakers. The developments in portable cameras and sound recording equipment, in the late 1950s, led to a documentary practice that was much more able to exploit the immediacy and 'behind-the-scenes' feel of social events and situations. One of the problems with this category of documentary is that it is often referred to in a shorthand way as *cinéma vérité* or, simply, *vérité* filmmaking. As the discussion of Jean Rouch and Edgar Morin's approach to documentary demonstrates (see below) however, *cinéma vérité* in its truest sense relies much more on filmmaker *intervention* (and interaction with their subjects) than does direct cinema. The confusion stems from the way that the term '*cinéma vérité*' has been used to describe what are actually very different approaches to documentary filmmaking. As Kevin MacDonald and Mark Cousins point out, *vérité* has now become a debased term, used to describe the 'look' of the film or programme 'rather than any genuine aspirations the filmmakers may have. As so often, what started as a revolution, has ended up a style choice' (1996: 251).

The poetic mode is one that eschews an explicit rhetorical or argumentative structure and favours associations of mood, tone, texture. Nichols states that 'the poetic mode sacrifices the conventions of continuity editing and the sense of a specific location in time and place that follows from it to explore [such] associations' (2001: 102). It has to be said that 'continuity editing' is hardly a feature of many documentaries, so it is unclear why it is used here as the 'norm' against which the poetic documentary is measured. However, it is certainly true that poetic documentaries may not have the rooted 'specificity' of other documentaries that use (for example) expository or observational approaches. Poetic documentaries have clear links to modernist and avant-garde movements in the ways that they foreground the often ephemeral and fragmented nature of subjectivity; rather than the apparent 'certainties' of expository and observational films, there is often an emphasis on the ambiguities of experience, and this can be seen as a form of commentary on the epistemological bases of documentary as a whole. The key to the poetic mode is that it is the aesthetic *expression* of aspects of the real that becomes the main focus, rather than the real *per se*. So, a 'city symphony' such as Walter Ruttmann's *Berlin: Symphony of a Great City* (1927, Ger.) uses images of that particular location within a framework of expressionist, rhythmic editing. Similarly, more recent films by Godfrey Reggio (for example *Koyaanisqatsi* (1983, US), *Powaqqatsi* (1988, US)) adopt a mesmeric montage style in order to construct a poetic, contemplative framework for images of the world.

The notion of the 'interactive' documentary privileges the interactions and relations between the filmmaker and that which they are filming. Instead of the 'neutral' detachment of the observational mode, or the didacticism of the expository mode (which is also 'detached', in its own way), we find active engagement and foregrounded exchange between people. Thus, the interactive documentary

> stresses images of testimony or verbal exchange ... textual author-
> ity [therefore] shifts towards the social actors recruited ... various
> forms of monologue and dialogue (real or apparent) predominate.
> (Nichols 1991: 44)

A key example here is the *cinéma vérité* of Rouch and Morin. In *Chronique d'un Ete* (*Chronicle of a Summer*, 1960, Fr.), Rouch and Morin develop a specific style that plays upon their role as filmmakers, and their ability to have an effect upon and shape the material they are filming. As some critics have made clear, this marks them out as very different from the American *vérité* practitioners (such as Leacock *et al.*, who should more accurately be described as direct cinema practitioners), because of the way Rouch and Morin view interaction between filmmaker and filmed as an intrinsically positive and productive thing.

> By appearing throughout the film, by seeking the active collabora-
> tion of the other participants, by overtly arranging and obviously
> handling the form of the film, Rouch and Morin are distinctly dif-
> ferent from the mainstream of American *vérité* filmmakers ... Drew,
> Leacock, Pennebaker and the Maysleses fear such involvement
> and interaction and believe that it would somehow contaminate
> the 'truth' believed to exist independently somewhere out there.
> Every effort is made in shooting and editing to have the filmmaker
> as invisible as possible and to assure the spectator that what he

> is seeing is in no way tampered with. It's 'the real thing'. For them, truth lies with the subject, not with the filmmaker. The camera is a recording device, a peephole. (Freyer 1979: 440)

Instead of a belief in filming events and people and the 'truth' of what is being filmed somehow emerging organically – something that the direct cinema practitioners professed to believe in – those who believe in a more 'interactive' style demonstrate that it is the filmmaker's input and 'manipulation' that is key.[3] This is not to suggest that this is *more* important than the actions of the 'subjects' – that would be to go too far the other way, and be equally wrong in its attempt to assert that one side of a dichotomy is 'more important' – what is vital is that we recognise the dialectical inter-relationship (that is, interaction) between what is filmed and who is doing the filming, the very processes of filming. A commonplace assertion about filming real people is that they will not 'be themselves'; that they will play up to the presence of the cameras. A key point is that this 'playing up' to the camera is not only unavoidable but should be actively embraced by filmmakers and critics. It is central to the notion of the 'performative' in documentary (see below) and should not be underestimated as a way of discovering truths about a specific situation or set of people.

In Mark Isaacs' short film *Lift* (2001, UK), for example, we can see a somewhat unconventional interview technique – a strange form of 'participant observation'. Isaacs spent one month in a tower block in the East End of London, where he would spend most of each day standing in the lift, holding a camera directed at the lift doors, filming whoever comes in to use the lift. Remaining silent at first, and not responding to the frankly bemused (and sometimes suspicious) responses of the inhabitants of the block, but instead 'merely' filming them, the documentary gradually develops into a more interview-based film. After deliberately not engaging with the people, Isaacs begins to ask questions, often out of the blue, such as 'What do you remember from your childhood?', 'Have you ever been in love?' Over the course of the 24-minute film, whilst we are clearly seeing a highly compressed and 'partial' view of (some of) these inhabitants, it builds up to give an original and strangely touching picture of these people and the place where they live. As a documentary, it is formally very interesting too, in the sense that it eschews any sense of showing the entirety of the environment – the wilful focusing on the interior of the lift magnifies

Figure 1 *Lift* (2001)

the small talk, silences, sidelong glances of this most interstitial of spaces. As Isaacs himself puts it: 'A lift is neither here nor there, people are waiting to get home or go out, and the longer I spent there the more able I was to ask the right questions.'[4]

While far from being a conventional documentary, *Lift* offers an intriguing insight into the world and the people it depicts. There are several wry jokes about a 'fly on the wall', when Isaacs cuts to a close up of a fly crawling up the wall of the lift; at the end of the film, the fly is shown expiring on the floor. The film therefore exhibits a humorous knowledge of viewer expectations about specific documentaries – one of the standard ways of presenting such 'social' material (the inhabitants of council estates, housing problems) would be in a fly-on-the-wall/observational style, and yet this film subverts that expectation. When the film begins, Isaacs assumes the role of detached observational filmmaker, there to simply film the comings and goings of various people in a particular milieu. Of course, the cramped, tiny space and his obvious presence militate against any such detached relationship with his subjects. This can be read as a deliberate ploy on Isaacs' part, to draw out with no little humour and irony some of the more outlandish claims to neutrality and objectivity made by the direct cinema practitioners. They (often explicitly) claimed to film things as they happen and literally capture the truth of the matter; Isaacs starts out trying to do this, and it quickly becomes apparent that it is a sham, as people *do* respond and react to his presence, and this is something that needs to be addressed. Of course, the space of the lift is used as a microcosm (with the emphasis on 'micro') of society, where people come and go, interacting with one another according to set rules. One day, a man with a movie camera happens to be there. Some people gamely try and ignore his presence – almost as if they have read a direct cinema 'rule book': 'just act naturally, and that means ignoring the camera!' But others gradually see this as a project in which they are partners (though not, perhaps, equal ones).

Some of the interactions with Isaacs are unprompted and seemingly a propos of nothing in particular. For example, one man turns and smiles at Isaacs/the camera hesitantly a few times before saying 'We've got a Jacuzzi in our flat.' When Isaacs says, off screen, 'I beg your pardon?' the man repeats this and elaborates, 'They're a lot bigger than you think. The flats, I mean.' We see the same man at various other points – cheerfully on his way out 'on the pull', drunkenly (but equally cheerfully) admitting he had got nowhere but had 'had a great night'. Other people are more reticent; others still even more outgoing. One Asian man keeps visiting the lift, even when not actually using it to travel up or down the tower block, with gifts of food for Isaacs. We also learn at one point that the majority of the inhabitants used to be Jewish, but now the 'white people' are in the minority. Such offhand comments could be construed as borderline racist (and perhaps the speakers are), but this is less a documentary that develops and explores these issues in any depth than one that recognises that they are important issues for many ordinary people out there; the sense of a changing social fabric, and people's differing attitudes towards it, are what is important here. Isaacs' somewhat eccentric style draws out these details in a way that would not happen in a more 'conventional' documentary. In many ways, the subject matter of *Lift* is how certain documentary conventions (and pretensions) might actually obscure the more interesting social truths about a situation. Isaacs begins the film a certain way, but then changes direction as his subjects do.[5]

This discussion of *Lift* has drawn attention to the fact that it is never easy to clearly and definitively state which single category a particular documentary might belong to (whilst nonetheless recognising that what one is watching *is* a documentary of some kind). Many documentaries use a range of techniques and strategies as suits their purpose. Even though the analysis here has tended to discuss *Lift* in terms of its 'interactive' or 'participatory' features, and especially the way that Isaacs playfully sends up these strategies, one could just as easily discuss the film in terms of its 'reflexivity', as it does (to an extent) reveal that it is a construction. The question of reflexivity in filmmaking is highly problematic. Generally speaking, it refers to the ways in which a filmmaker might somehow reveal the filmmaking process itself, as the text unfolds. As such a manoeuvre can (indeed, *should*, if it is working properly) unsettle the spectator's expectations and assumptions, it can be an interesting political strategy. To be reflexive in any medium is to engage in a metacommentary, or a commentary on the processes of representation themselves. As Nichols puts it, while 'most documentary production concerns itself with talking about the historical world, the reflexive mode addresses the question of *how* we talk about the historical world' (1991: 56–7, emphasis in original). (This is an important issue and forms the basis of the discussion of *The Battle of Orgreave* in chapter three). One of the problems here is that notions of reflexivity are often misunderstood to merely be formal and stylistic in nature – to do with surface features of the text. In my teaching of documentary practice I have often found that students will assume that merely by showing someone holding a camera or other item of kit, 'behind the scenes' (for example the Broomfield-esque boom microphone), they are somehow 'being reflexive'. The assumption seems to be that by showing (to *any* extent) that what we are watching has been filmed and constructed, the viewer will magically understand the importance of this fact. As Nichols goes on to point out though, 'reflexive texts are self-conscious not only about form and style ... but also about strategy, structure, conventions, expectations and effects' (ibid.). In other words, proper reflexivity involves an understanding of the social implications and consequences of revealing that something is a construction; anything less than this runs the risk of a self-regarding solipsism.

The main problem with reflexivity is that first of all it is often simplistically entangled with questions of (scepticism about) objectivity, and secondly it seems assumed that reflexivity will magically guarantee a deeper truthfulness and profundity. This explains why some student productions sprinkle 'reflexive' tropes over their documentary like so much seasoning: they have misunderstood the purpose and the reasons for reflexivity in the first place. As Noël Carroll has argued, this entanglement of reflexivity with questioning objectivity is an inevitable consequence of certain stances on nonfiction texts. If a film does *not* use reflexive strategies it is upbraided for 'denying' the fact that it is a construction, and this, in turn, means that suspicion is cast on *any* claims it might make to say something about the real world. As Carroll asks '[does] *not calling attention to* such construction processes amount to *denying* the existence of those processes?' (1996: 293, emphasis in original). He thinks not: 'Denial, so to say, is its own speech act. In denying something, one generally has to do something. It doesn't simply happen that I deny my heritage if I ask someone to pass me the pepper without telling them I'm Irish' (ibid.). In short, the only way to *deny* that a specific documentary is a constructed artefact would be to state in some shape or form during the course of the documentary 'This is not a constructed artefact'. But – in the same way as Magritte's *The Betrayal of Images*, an image of a pipe with the legend 'Ceci n'est pas une pipe' ['This is not a pipe'] – such denial does nothing more than draw attention to the process of representation it seeks to deny; it is, in effect, a reflexive strategy.

The way out of this conundrum is simply to recognise that much of the scepticism about the 'fictiveness' of documentary, or the problems of (non-)reflexivity, is a red herring. People can and do routinely recognise that what they are watching is 'fictional', 'nonfictional' or some kind of hybrid. The fact that there are a vast number of differently inflected hybrids – from drama-documentaries, to 'based on'/true-life stories, to reality TV, standard expository documentaries, re-enactments of some shape or form – does not mean that people cannot at least attempt to discern where a specific text 'fits'. There are admittedly some cases where what one is viewing *is* indeterminate – the film *No Lies* (Mitchell Block, 1973, US), for example, or *The Day Britain Stopped* (Gabriel Range, 2003, UK) – but it is the indeterminacy that is part of the point of such examples. As such, it is an intrinsic 'talking point' about them. For example, virtually every newspaper article, review or radio discussion of *The Day Britain Stopped* referred explicitly to its frighteningly accurate simulation of broadcast news reports and its piecing together of what appears to be a standard contemporary history documentary. The idea that any viewers were really, truly duped into thinking that these events had actually happened is an urban myth; a myth that raises all sorts of interesting debating points about documentary representation, ethics and the role of fabrication – but a myth all the same. We need a more sophisticated notion of how spectators engage with documentary texts of varying kinds, as all too often it appears that the viewer is posited as someone who has not a clue about the world they inhabit, nor the standard modes of representation that they routinely encounter. We shall return to some of these issues of documentary spectatorship.

The notion of the 'performative' documentary is a very complex area, and is something discussed in more detail in the next chapter, when documentaries where real people 'play themselves' are examined, as well as the representational problems raised by different 'versions' of the 'same' story (the main example being the Aileen Wuornos story). For the moment, it is sufficient to say that many performative documentaries could also be discussed under the previous heading of reflexive, in the sense that they foreground the subjective and self-conscious aspects of the documentary filmmaker and/or their subjects. It is this subjective discourse that Nichols emphasises in his definition of the 'performative mode' (1994: 92–106). Bruzzi objects to this as too simplistic, and says that discussion of the performative documentary can and should usefully follow the linguistic theory of J. L. Austin, where 'performative' refers to 'utterances that simultaneously both describe and perform an action' (2000: 154). The central thesis of Bruzzi's book is that 'documentaries are a negotiation between filmmaker and reality and, at heart, a performance' (ibid.) and she further states that documentaries that are specifically referred to as 'performative' are 'the enactment of the notion that a documentary only comes into being as it is performed ... although its factual basis (or document) can pre-date any recording or representation of it, the film is necessarily performative because it is given meaning by the interaction between performance and reality' (ibid.).

As the extended glossing of his categories suggests, it appears reasonable to agree with Nichols that the proposing of modes and typologies, or attempts to *categorise* certain practices, is a very useful thing to do. In disagreeing with some of Nichols' points or conclusions, some of his critics appear to go overboard and reject the categories themselves. As we shall see below, however, the discursive categories we create in order to understand what something is and how it works actually have a defining power over that something. How we talk about things impacts upon those things. Bruzzi takes issue with Nichols' categorising and typologies, and especially what she sees as his 'evolutionary' or 'genealogical' construction of documentary history; although the categories proposed by Nichols are very useful, one can agree with Bruzzi that any suggestion of them being in a chronological relationship is misleading. Nichols has pointed out that they co-exist and do not 'replace' each other, but this is not precise enough and what is needed is a model where there are different modes of documentary practice, but that they are seen as dialectically inter-related. Certainly one can trace trends and tendencies, where one specific type of documentary discourse (for example the expository) might be seen to dominate a specific era or culture. But there have always been so-called 'reflexive' documentaries, and there continue to be 'expository' documentaries in the present. It is more to do with how these modes are taken up and used in specific contexts that is of interest – and this can be perceived as a type of 'hybridity' in documentary – rather than looking for 'new' modes. We have discussed *Lift*, for example, in a way that emphasises its ironic juxtaposition of modes: it is not so much that we can point to this film and say it is startlingly 'new' (though it *is* refreshingly eccentric and original); its strength lies in the way that Isaacs playfully deals with a well-trodden pathway, using a deliberate and self-conscious mixture of modes. As we shall see in later chapters, the most diverse of documentary practices will use a range of exposition, observation and overt 'reflexive' comment as suits their purposes at any particular time. It is also the case that it is people's active engagement with these practices that actually constitute what we understand documentary to be at any particular moment. It is important therefore that we examine the range of ways in which documentary is talked about and understood, and the importance of categories, modes and types.

Boundaries, prototypes and communities of practice

The main problem for those examining documentary is that it is too often thought of in essentialist terms. In other words, the assumption seems to be that there is somewhere 'out there', the 'model' or 'typical' documentary, against which all attempts at documentary are measured. Documentary worth is more often than not equated with an ideal of 'transparency' and 'objectivity'. Such criteria clearly stem from the dominance of a specific type of documentary – the aforementioned American direct cinema of practitioners such as Pennebaker, the Maysles Brothers, Drew and Leacock. The legacy of direct cinema is such that most of the 'commonsense' things that are said about 'documentary' actually only really refer to films from the direct cinema stable. The main difficulty is the way that essentialist notions of documentary limit the development and understanding of the form: the features of a *certain type* of documentary come to stand for the *whole* of documentary, in what we could term a metonymic relationship. If someone were to suggest that all fiction films had to be musicals, or talked about musicals as if they were the only type of fiction film against which all others should be measured,[6] then they would be dismissed as being unduly prescriptive, as holding up what is actually *one type* of something as if it is the *only* type. Or, rather, that it is the central, most important type, and all others are *deviations* from it. Yet this is what appears to happen routinely when discussing documentaries: certain features of some documentaries are held up as of central importance, and if a film does not contain them (or, if it deliberately flouts them), then its status as a documentary is thereby doubted.

Carl Plantinga (1997) has written usefully about documentary, suggesting that thinking in terms of 'prototypical' examples, and those that are less typical, is a helpful way forward. He argues that documentary is an 'open concept' with 'fuzzy boundaries', and that the full range of documentary expression can only be understood if we engage with the notion of categorisation. How we talk about and categorise things has a meaningful impact on those very things. Language and ways of understanding the world are social phenomena, subject to change, and it is this changeability that needs to be incorporated into any useful model for categorising and understanding documentary.

Plantinga writes about documentary as a form of the broader category, nonfiction, and borrows Noël Carroll's concept of 'indexing' to understand how such films operate in the social sphere. While making clear that there is 'no necessary realism or resemblance between the nonfiction work and actuality' (1997: 18), he also argues that any fundamental distinction we make between fiction and nonfiction is based on this notion of indexing and the response of the spectator – in other words, the contextual factors. What he means by this is that a nonfiction film can diverge from a mere slavish imitation of actuality – that is, it could be 'stylised' in some shape or form – but will still be 'understood' as nonfictional by its spectators. Obviously, this is a complex area, and certain very specific types of film and television programme deliberately play upon this notion of indexing. For example, the varying kinds of 'mock-documentary', spoofs and the like, take the recognisable conventions of this kind of discourse, and use the spectators' engagement to sustain their effect. So, *This is Spinal Tap* (Rob Reiner, 1984, US), or the BBC series *The Office* derive their comedic effects from our recognition of specific documentary conventions. This notion of 'recognition' is especially important when we come to talk about documentary canons, and works that are deemed to deviate from what is the 'norm' for documentary. As we shall see, such 'deviation' is actually what keeps the form alive and developing, but it is required that practitioners and audiences recognise it in a very specific way.

To this end, we need to think about classification and categorisation as *material* practices – that is, practices that have actual real-world consequences – as it is in this realm that norms, standards, conventions and deviations are (more often than not, *implicitly*) understood. Geoffrey C. Bowker and Susan Leigh Star (1999) have done some interesting work on classification and its consequences, and anyone thinking about documentary as a category needs to take on board some of what they say. It is precisely because documentary is a so-called 'open concept' that we need a *flexible* way of understanding how such a diverse set of texts 'fit together'. Bowker and Star start by offering definitions of the terms 'classification' and 'standards' (1999: 10–16). They define a 'classification' as 'a spatial, temporal, or spatio-temporal segmentation of the world' further stating that 'in an ideal, abstract sense' a classification system is consistent, has categories that are clearly mutually exclusive, and that the system is complete or 'provides total coverage of the world it describes'. They also acknowledge, quite correctly, that 'no real-world working classification system ... meets these "simple" requirements and we doubt that any ever could' (1999: 11). Nevertheless, it is in the ways that we *negotiate* whether or not something 'fits' that we are constantly made to reappraise the things themselves and the categories. For example, it is commonplace when an innovation takes place in an area that some people are uncomfortable with or reject it. The recent phenomena of 'reality TV' and 'docu-soaps' are a prime example of this – they are denigrated for 'dumbing down' the documentary ideal, going a fabrication too far in their pursuit of zany characters and (more to the point) high ratings. These things might very well be true in certain instances (but they are not necessarily true across the board), but that is beside the point. The most important thing is that such innovations mean we have to re-think commonly-held beliefs about what 'documentary' is and where it might be going. To simply say, then, that a programme like *Big Brother* is 'not documentary' strikes me as facile: all anyone is saying if they state this is that *Big Brother* is not *their idea* of a documentary (and they will usually be measuring 'documentary' by the 'Griersonian' informa-tive/educational model, or that of the 'observational' direct cinema model, and their variants). *Big Brother* might involve people playing up to the cameras, performing, pretending – but so do many other documentaries. It is far more important to discuss the reasons why some people think that certain texts are 'not documentary' (or 'not *proper* documentary') than it is to posit intractable, essentialist notions of what constitutes the form.

However, this raises two very important points. First of all, that cat-egories and the norms associated with them are social constructs and are therefore only meaningful if people broadly *agree* on their usage. As Plantinga points out (1997: 19–20) things are often 'named according to their conventional functions, and an unconventional use of an artifact does not require that we change its name' – his example being if someone uses a toaster as a weapon to hit an intruder, it would still be described as a 'toaster', despite its unconventional usage on that particular occasion. A similar conventional usage prevents someone from simply understand-ing a fictional film as nonfictional (or vice versa): if we were to watch *The Matrix* (Andy and Larry Wachowski, 1999, US) as nonfiction we would be misunderstanding the film's status.[7] Secondly, the idea of a *negotiated* consensus on what constitutes a 'documentary' suggests that there are different constituencies out there in the world, contesting what this might mean. Critical discourse on 'reality TV' often suggests that it is a debased version of the documentary ideal. A number of reviewers of Michael Moore's polemical films, such as *Roger and Me* (1989, US), *Bowling for Columbine* (2000, US) or *Fahrenheit 9/11* (2003, US), take him to task for what they perceive to be his overt manipulations and journalistic shortcom-ings. Such critical positions are of course predicated on some yardstick of 'documentariness' against which these examples come up short for those particular critics.

This brings us to the notion of 'standards', and how they impact upon and shape the different 'communities of practice'. As Bowker and Star point out, a standard is 'any set of agreed-upon rules for the production of (textual or material) objects ... [it] spans more than one community of practice (or site of activity)' (1999: 13). The problem we have with an open concept or category such as documentary is that there appears to be a number of conflicting ideas of what constitutes the field – in other words, perhaps there is no 'standard'? This is not really the case, but in saying this we do need to emphasise the fact that supposed standards will be read differently and adapted according to context. This is not the same as saying 'anything goes', but rather that different documentarists will approach things in different ways to suit their purposes. To take a key example: there is no one single way of conducting and presenting an interview. To say that there is a 'standard' relating to interviews should not mean (in a commonsense way) that there is a 'standard' way of *doing* the interview. This is not what different documentarists will agree about. What they will agree about is that interview material (of varying types and approaches) is vitally important to documentary as a mode. In *this* sense, it is a 'standard' of documentary practice. But this should not be taken to mean, as some critics implicitly do, that there should be a 'preferred' way of doing interviews.[8]

One of the ways that we can understand how seemingly diverse and multi-sited people might be said to all be doing the 'same' thing (in this case, making documentaries) is to use Jean Lave and Etienne Wenger's term, 'legitimate peripheral participation', something they talk about in relation to what they term 'situated learning' and 'communities of practice' (1991). Their perspective is one that sees learning as an intrinsically social process, rather than the simple 'transmission' of facts from one person to another. Legitimate peripheral participation refers to the ways that individuals learn in a 'socially situated' manner, and how communities of practice are sustained across a wide range of contexts and groups. Interaction and engagement is not a static thing or a simple 'exchange' but is something that is in flux and any learning and communication that occurs is 'socially situated':

Legitimate peripheral participation provides a way to speak about the relations between newcomers and old-timers, and about activities, identities, artifacts and communities of knowledge and practice. It concerns the process by which newcomers become part of the community of practice. A person's intentions to learn are engaged and the meaning of learning is configured through the process of becoming a full participant in a sociocultural practice. (1991: 29)

In other words, people will orient themselves to specific knowledges by relating what *they* do and think to what *others* – perceived to be 'already there', 'in the know' – do and think. In terms of documentary practice, there is a clear correlation in the sense that people will make films and programmes that follow specific conventional structures, or they will endeavour to subvert these, or create interesting hybrids, and so on. The docu-soap, the mock-documentary, the video diary – all of these are types of documentary that borrow from and bend the rules of specific sets of conventions, and they first appeared as innovations in form – or 'peripheral' or 'marginal' to what was then 'mainstream' documentary. They have gradually moved to become more central, such that the docu-soap format, for example, is now seen as a highly orthodox part of the television schedules. It is this dynamic relationship between the perceived centre and the perceived margins that we shall now explore via a discussion of documentary canons.

Documentary canons and margins

As noted above, Bruzzi identifies a tendency in the work of Bill Nichols – what she refers to as his 'family tree' of documentary modes. It is certainly true that suggesting that the development of documentary is in any way a tidy, chronological 'evolution' is highly problematic. However, this does not totally invalidate the usefulness of the categories or modes that Nichols suggests. We can point out, as Bruzzi does, that the expository mode was not *superseded* by the interactive or reflexive modes, that it still exists today, or that many early documentaries were imaginatively reflexive and far from the didacticism associated with the expository mode (see, for example, Vertov's *Man with a Movie Camera*). Nevertheless, as this overview implies, the modes that Nichols proposes are broadly useful, especially when used in conjunction with Bruzzi's suggestion that all documentaries must be seen as a dialectical relationship between the events depicted and their mode of depiction.

Another most useful issue that Bruzzi addresses is that of a 'canon' of documentary films which are held up as exemplary. Of course, the only way we can propose an argument about documentary is by recourse to examples, but the problem has tended to be that certain types of documentary have become so dominant that it skews things so that we end up with the metonymic relationship mentioned earlier. Thus, the 'Griersonian' social documentary of the 1930s, direct cinema in the US in the 1950 and 1960s and more recently – and more contentiously – notions of 'reality TV' and docu-soaps are all held up as models of 'documentariness', ones that capture the spirit of a particular moment. The problem with a canon is that it implies 'norms' in the sense that the films in the canon exhibit certain features and tendencies; any that do not measure up to these yardsticks are placed 'outside' the canon. This is not a wilful attempt to shed light on obscure or completely overlooked documentaries but rather to suggest, as Plantinga does, that we need to think carefully about the *whole spectrum* of documentary activity. As the category work done by Bowker and Star (or George Lakoff's prototype theory, to which Plantinga alludes) suggests, categorising is an apparently unavoidable way that humans make sense of the world. At the same time, though, we should remember that categories are potentially mobile in the way suggested by Lave and Wenger's work on 'communities of practice'. A documentary's meaningfulness might alter depending on who is watching it, in what context, and for what purpose. For example, a 1930s information film can be the source of much unintended amusement for a twenty-first-century audience, due to the stilted re-enactments, and dated social graces. This brings us full circle to the notion of the meaning of a documentary being a process of negotiation between the film, the filmmaker, their audience(s) and the social and viewing context. The importance of spectatorship for documentary studies cannot be overstated, and is increasingly recognised; we can therefore conclude this chapter by introducing some of the central issues in this area, as they will inform discussion in subsequent chapters.

The role of the viewer in deciphering, interpreting and categorising different types of documentary is now central to any convincing critical framework on the subject. As the points above on communities of practice, standards and canons intimate, there is a constant discursive dimension to anyone's understanding of documentary output. With the increased 'hybridisation' of the form – so much so that arguably the term 'documentary' has lost much of its descriptive power in any case – the interpretative activity of the audience is paramount. There are clear instances where the spectator is placed in a position that highlights the very act of spectating, and all the claims to knowledgeability that this implies. For example, many 'reflexive' documentaries will draw attention to the uncertainties and gaps in their discourse, and foreground the processes of meaning construction; the point of such strategies is arguably to make the viewer critically reflect on their role in interpreting the material. In *Capturing the Friedmans* (Andrew Jarecki, 2003, US), for instance, the role of the viewer is vitally important for the filmmaker's techniques to work (see Austin 2005b). The film does not 'give us the truth' of what happened, but asks us to think about and evaluate what we are told. There is an explicit emphasis on the importance of the film's spectators (this is stated a number of times in interviews with Jarecki and post-screening audience discussions, included on the DVD release of the film).

Figure 2 *Capturing the Friedmans* (2003)

Such emphasis on the viewer's (inevitably) subjective interpretation of what a documentary is 'about' does have its limits, however. As Plantinga makes clear, the logical conclusion of 'subjectivist' theories of film is a strange state of affairs where 'the viewer actually defines and constructs the text within the process of viewing' (2000: 133). While this can be seen as a corrective to theories that suggest that some kind of 'ideal' spectator is constructed and positioned by the text, the truth of the matter is somewhere in between. As the discussion above of 'conventional usage' suggested, it is not in the power of individual spectators to decide whether what they are watching is 'fiction' or 'nonfiction'; this is something that is *socially* negotiated. As will be argued in subsequent chapters, the changing form and function of texts that appear to have some documentary intention (and here we can include things like mock-documentaries, or films that consist of entirely dramatised reconstructions or re-enactments) mean that the burden of active viewing is placed on the spectator. Now, more than ever, it seems that we are repeatedly being asked to make decisions as to the ontological basis of what we are watching – that is, ask ourselves '*is this a documentary?*'

Dai Vaughan talks of the 'documentary response' from the spectator in relation to certain material; 'documentary' as a term describes 'not a style or method or a genre of filmmaking but a mode of response to film material' (1999: 58). In short, viewers will respond to material in a way that recognises its direct relationship to actuality. Such a response does not mean that viewers will watch something and take it as a direct *record* of some aspect of actuality, but that they will recognise and understand that the film or programme in question is attempting to make assertions about that actuality. This is why viewers can have a legitimate 'documentary response' to animated documentaries or dramatised reconstructions: whilst problematic if viewed as direct, indexically-linked recordings of actuality, such films ask the viewer to respond in a certain manner, and it is this that gives them their documentary status. In the next chapter, we shall examine the relationship between drama and documentary, with a view to clarifying what happens when these modes meet.

2   FICTION AND NONFICTION: THE GREAT DIVIDE?

'Seldom any splendid story is wholly true.'
                                        – Samuel Johnson

One of the most interesting things in studying the documentary field is the complex relationship between fiction, nonfiction and documentary as categories, and how they overlap. A commonsense assumption, for example, appears to be that any use of narrative or dramatisation is somehow equal to fictionalising, and that this effectively negates any documentary worth that a film might have. As noted in the previous chapter however, central to an understanding of 'documentary' is the spectatorial activity of actually interpreting the material, something that Dai Vaughan has discussed as the 'documentary response' (1999), and Noël Carroll has suggested comes under the rubric of a system of 'indexing' (1996). And, as will be argued in this chapter via a series of case studies, the relationship between fiction and nonfiction is increasingly what Bill Nichols (1994) would describe as a 'blurred boundary'. As we shall see (in this chapter and, subsequently, in chapter three) use of a narrative or even certain supposedly 'fictional' techniques – such as reconstruction or re-enactment – is by no means out of bounds for the documentarist. Indeed, some of the more interesting work in the area has always been that which explores the boundary between these apparently 'separate' modes.

In chapter three we shall specifically examine the different ways that various films have used re-enactment and reconstruction with a view to mapping how documentaries engage with history and constructions of the past. This chapter will first of all offer an outline of some the critical debates relating to drama and documentary as seemingly separate, yet complexly overlapping modes. It will then move on to examine how some specific examples tell their stories, from what perspective, and what consequences this has for their perceived status as 'documentary'. The inter-relationships between drama documentary, documentary drama (and all the variations on these) have always been complex, and they have become much more so in recent times. One of the key areas to be examined will be the ways in which actors perform the role of real people in reconstructed or re-enacted scenes, and, more contentiously, how real people/non-actors 'play themselves' in some way. These modalities of performance clearly strike right to the heart of a 'traditional' (and some would say hopelessly outdated) 'documentariness' in the sense that they foreground the hybrid and uncertain nature of much contemporary documentary output. In other words, our ways of understanding what is going on in current documentary production (and criticism) needs to take on board the increasingly blurred boundary between fiction and nonfiction, acting and simply being. The final part of the chapter will examine what may be seen as one of the more interesting recent phenomena in documentary, the Aileen Wuornos affair. There are two Nick Broomfield documentaries about Wuornos and the strange people who associated with her in her last years, but rather than simply offering a reading of these documentaries, here we shall explore the relationship between these films and the other dramatised/fictionalised versions of the Wuornos story. Rather than seeing the documentaries as the more 'authentic' and 'truthful' version of 'what really happened', this area is opened up so that the complex web of meanings created by all texts pertaining to the Wuornos story can be seen as part of how we understand it; there are issues around fiction and reality, performance and deception that can usefully be interrogated by looking at the relationships between these different versions of the 'same' story.

Drama and documentary as modes

Derek Paget (1990; 1998) has done much interesting work that attempts to tease out some of the intricacies of the relationship between 'documentary' and 'drama' as terms. Paget uses a 'wordsearch' approach, stating that 'the phrases, compound nouns and noun-coinages in question [when discussing "drama" and "documentary" and their inter-relatedness] are drawn mainly from four root words – "documentary", "drama", "fact" and "fiction"' (1998: 90–1). He then goes on to map a tentative list of terms and phrases that are in common usage (some more common than others). For example, there are those terms that use both 'drama' and 'documentary', but lead off with the former – so we have 'dramatised documentary', 'drama documentary', 'drama-documentary' and 'dramadoc'. Paget also states that 'dramatic reconstruction' can be included in this list as the term reconstruction identifies 'a documentary claim' (1998: 91). Next, there are those terms that combine the same two terms but lead with 'documentary': 'documentary drama', 'documentary-drama', 'docudrama' or 'documentary-style' all fall into this section. Lastly, there are those terms that do not necessarily directly use either 'drama' or 'documentary', but play on some sense of 'fact' and 'fiction' to draw out much the same tension as the other categories: 'faction', 'fact-based drama', 'based on fact', or 'based on a true story' are the key examples here.

There are, of course, considerable problems with all of these terms in that they are often used so interchangeably as to lose specificity in their meaning. Again, as Paget makes clear, the key confusion is between those terms that use 'drama' and 'documentary' as their foundations – it is commonplace to see the same film or programme referred to as both a 'drama documentary' *and* a 'documentary drama', as if there is no difference between them. Is there a difference? Paget's contention that we think about where the *relative* emphasis lies is certainly a useful one:

> It is tempting to regard the phrases ... as always weighted towards the second word. Thus, just as 'dramatic' in the phrase 'dramatic documentary' acts as an adjective modifying the noun 'documentary', so 'drama documentary' is a documentary treated dramatically. But 'drama-documentary' claims a balance in which, perhaps, both will be equally present. (1998: 93)

Although this is useful up to a point, the problem remains of how we define when something is being 'treated dramatically'; this is especially problematic now that we have a range of hybridised documentary output that has moved beyond the apparently simpler demarcations of 'drama' and 'documentary' (and these boundaries were never that clear-cut in the first place). These new hybrids (or what Paget has referred to as 'not-docs' in a work-in-progress article (2002)) are ones that deliberately flaunt or distort their relative use of 'documentary', 'drama', 'fact' and 'fiction' to the extent that the viewer is less than certain as to what they are watching.[1] Rather than the clear-cut, easily-identifiable modes of conventional documentary – real people in real situations – these texts tend to use adapted conventions – real people in reconstructions, actors playing real people in documentary re-enactments – in order to make their points. These (and other) shifts in documentary signification have led John Corner (2000) to talk tentatively of a 'post-documentary' era, where hybridisation and what he identifies as a tendency towards 'documentary as diversion' are the main driving forces. As with any impulse towards using 'dramatised' forms (reconstructions and the like) there are always very good reasons for building a documentary around reconstructed or re-enacted material. Either there is no 'direct' record of the events that can simply be drawn into the documentary context – this is the case with events from history when no cameras were present – or there are issues around anonymity or other problems with access that mean that reconstruction is one of the only options available.

Re-enacting the real: the performing of real-life scenarios

In her discussion of an edition of the BBC current affairs programme *Panorama* about the serial killer Dr Harold Shipman (*Dr Shipman: The Man Who Played God*, 2000, UK) – a programme that made extensive use of dramatised reconstructions of Shipman's murders – Catherine Bennett (2000) tends to overstate some of the issues and problems relating to reconstruction, concluding that it is a completely invalid strategy: 'Acknowledged reconstructions do not deceive ... but they short-change us, deal in a currency inferior to the truth.' Increasingly, documentarists are using techniques that clearly fall within the boundaries of 'reconstruction', but they are doing so in a way that is more complex than Bennett appears to allow, as she sees all reconstruction as essentially *fictional*. A key factor for consideration in documentary and non-fiction is of course that the events and persons depicted exist (or did exist) in the real world of actuality. Whereas in a fiction film, the events and persons are precisely that – fictional or made up. There are some interesting ways in which these apparently very simple demarcations are complicated, however. First and foremost, as sketched out above, we can talk of the various types of 'dramatised' documentary, where 'drama' and 'documentary' as modes are perceived to play off one another in some shape or form. These distinctions between documentary, drama-documentary and documentary-drama (and all the various points in between) are interesting and have been discussed at some length elsewhere. The immediate interest here is to examine some of the ways that recent film and programme makers have engaged with the notion of representing apparently real-world events, but do so by using dramatised forms of reconstruction and performance. The matter, as with much these days in the realm of documentary, is far from cut and dried.

In *Tina Goes Shopping* (Penny Woolcock, 1999, UK) and its sequel *Tina Takes a Break* (Penny Woolcock, 2001, UK) the events depicted take place on an impoverished Leeds housing estate. The film begins with a 'continuity announcer'-style voiceover, speaking over a montage of split-screen scenes from the film itself. The voice explains Woolcock's working methods and places the events we are about to see in some sort of documentary context:

> She spent the next twelve months getting to know the inhabitants of some of the toughest estates in Leeds. She collected accounts of real events witnessed by the characters in their own lives and with them she shaped a drama. In the film, the residents improvise the story in their own words; no one is playing themselves, but it's a world they know only too well.

The film is an improvised, highly naturalistic drama based on stories that are purported to have actually happened. As a caption says just after the opening sequence, 'This is a drama inspired by true stories'. What is interesting here is how such a documentary drama format gives us access to material that we would not otherwise see. The main example here is Tina herself (played by Kelly Hollis). The eponymous character runs what she calls a 'shopping service': she takes orders from her friends and neighbours and then pilfers the items on a shoplifting spree. We see her doing this and freely admitting to it in a way that would not happen in a conventional documentary. For example, in one of the shoplifting scenes, we see Tina removing security tags from items of clothing she is about to steal. As she does this, she says to the camera, 'The difference between "grafting" and "grafters" is that *this* is grafting – what you *have* to do – and grafters go out to work legally.' There are some similar voiceovers or frank straight-to-camera admissions by other characters in the film – Aaron, Tina's crack-addict boyfriend, or Don, her drug-dealing father – people admitting to things in a way that they never would in a conventional documentary.

Clearly then, these films are not 'documentary' in a straightforward sense of the term, as they involve people 'acting' and improvising, playing characters other than themselves. However, there is an argument that *all* documentary (and, indeed, all social interaction) involves people 'acting' in some sense of the term, so the distinction is arguably a matter of degree rather than us talking about completely different things. It is certainly the case that all manner of reality TV programmes rely on participants with a highly developed sense of performance. For example, the makers of a docu-soap will actively seek out flamboyant 'characters' in the (undoubt-edly correct) belief that it will boost ratings. A programme such as *Big Brother* similarly relies on the contestants being 'entertaining' and play-ing to the cameras, juxtaposed with the more confessional/video diary conventions of the diary-room sequences. At the time of writing Makosi, a contestant in *Big Brother 6*, has been given several 'secret missions' by Big Brother, where she has had to lie, cheat and steal from fellow housemates. This has led to inevitable arguments and accusations that she is 'not being herself'; another housemate has even entertained thoughts that Makosi may be a 'mole', placed in the house by Big Brother. The point of this is that the issues of performance and deception that are played out in these *Big Brother* scenarios are something that are central to a great deal of recent factual programming and documentary hybrids. In certain cases – for exam-ple, the infamous case of Carlton TV's programme *The Connection* (1996), which included certain scenes of drug dealing that were dramatic recon-structions, but were passed off by the programme makers as the real thing captured then and there – the audience has been duped, pure and simple. But in other cases, we are seeing something more complex and nuanced than simple out-and-out 'deception'. The fact that we are watching actors performing in a reconstruction is more often than not flagged up, and the wider questions being asked here are therefore to do with the status of 'performance' in contemporary factual television and filmmaking.

That aside, we need to think carefully about the status of films like *Tina Goes Shopping*. They 'document' a real, social reality in an utterly com-pelling way, and reveal things about their respective social contexts and characters that a 'conventional' documentary would arguably never be able to. The difficulty is that if these films are rejected out of hand as unable to usefully 'document' an aspect of reality, simply because they are a kind of improvised drama, then certain aspects of reality will never adequately be represented. It is the ability of such films as *Tina Goes Shopping* to show the reality of certain parts of society from 'within', as it were; that is their strength.

Another key example of this tendency was an edition of *Panorama* on the children of drug addicts, *The Invisible Kids* (2004, UK). All of the words were spoken by actors, yet the testimony given was drawn directly, word for word, from that given by real children living with this problem. Similarly, in the Channel 4 film *Pissed on the Job* (2004, UK), we were given detailed glimpses into the lives of some 'high-functioning alcoholics' (that is, people who are addicted to alcohol but manage to hold down responsible jobs). Here we have the real testimony of real people talking about their problem. The only way one could do this in a conventional documentary is to use the 'silhouette' technique, and/or disguise the voice of the person, such are the negative connotations for someone in such a position being an alcoholic. Such a technique, used for an entire film, might be deemed to be problematic for the filmmakers (as it would be a turn-off for the viewers). So, we have actors playing the roles, shot in a highly naturalistic style, interspersing direct-to-camera interviews (with the actor-as-alcoholic talking to an off-camera interviewer) with apparent reconstructions of events from their lives.

In all of the above examples, we clearly are being asked to take 'as documentary' something that is 'performed' by actors (in the case of *Tina Goes Shopping*, they are real people/non-actors, but they are playing roles). This is not to imply that we are duped (though this may of course be the case), but it is to stress that these films actively play upon the 'uncertainty' of the images and sounds they contain. Some commentators might simply dismiss them as out-and-out dramas, fabulations, but apart from anything else, they offer us access to parts of the real world we might not otherwise see (at least not in the depth and detail afforded us here). So some serious thought needs to be given to the truth status of what we see and hear in these films. This notion of how such acted dramas can have a documentary or 'truth' value is something returned to below via the discussion of the various versions of the Aileen Wuornos story.

Returning to the distinctions mapped out above, we cannot say that the stories told in *Pissed on the Job* or *Tina Goes Shopping* are 'fictional' in the accepted sense of them being fabricated. Neither are they 'merely' stories with a highly naturalistic gloss: both are based on the real experiences of real people. In the case of *Pissed on the Job*, the film's basis is a series of confidential interviews with the real people. The events they have talked about are then reconstructed and their actions performed by actors. The film takes the form of a series of intercut 'case studies' with high-functioning alcoholics: we are introduced to each character in turn, seeing them first of all talking to an off-screen (and unheard) interviewer. Each character represents a 'sector' of society – there is a schoolteacher, a doctor, a nanny, a London Underground station manager, a housewife/mother – so that their 'personal' problem becomes indicative of a wider social issue. It is important that the people cast in these roles are unknown (or little-known) actors so that such a 'social problem' moment can be played out;[2] if the people were played by clearly recognisable actors (or stars), then the effect would be diminished. In any case, it is difficult to say where, exactly, such a programme might 'fit' in terms of commonsense notions of 'drama documentary' and all the variations noted above. Clearly, the intention is to 'document' a specific social issue, and to do so by using the testimony of real people as the foundation for what is said. The 'same' issue could have been explored via a realist, fictional film – for example the Hollywood film *When a Man Loves a Woman* (Luis Mandoki, 1994, US) examines how alcoholism impacts upon a specific family's life – but the problems and issues are explored – and, crucially, resolved – in very different ways in such narratives. *Pissed on the Job* is not simply 'dramatised' documentary (or 'documentarised' drama). One could argue, for the sake of simplicity, that it is in a 'documentary style', but I think this is too vague a category (after all, how many 'styles' of documentary are there?). The programme exists on a boundary between conventional nonfictional address and the range of other modalities that bubble to the surface when we consider what happens when one person speaks the words of another, or a set of filmmakers reconstitute and re-enact a particular slice of actuality.

In any case, despite their apparent 'non-documentariness' for some people, such films as *Pissed on the Job* or the *Tina* films are no more or no less problematic for a definition of documentary than were the films

Grierson and his associates made some sixty years previously. As Brian Winston has argued, there is a considerable history to 'reconstruction' in documentary, and the techniques associated with reconstruction were widespread in the 'Griersonian' tradition of documentary filmmaking (1995: 120–3). The notion that 'judicious' or 'sincere and justifiable' reconstruction could (indeed, *had to*) take place in documentary was something that was broadly accepted. This was partly to do with the limitations of the time in that the simplest approach of filming with synch sound on location (what became the basis of the direct cinema approach) was at that point not possible. Intervention and fabrication of material that commonly existed in actuality was therefore often the only way (the filmmakers thought) of bringing certain things to the screen. Thus, what would in the contemporary moment be presented as a 'video diary' or 'docu-soap' – using location shooting and synch sound – was in Grierson's day routinely 'mocked up' and reconstructed. *Night Mail* (Harry Watt and Basil Wright, 1936, UK), for example, famously reconstructed the sorting coach of the train. In a similar way, the story of *A Job in a Million* (Evelyn Cherry, 1937, UK) is told via a

Figure 3 *Night Mail* (1936)

frankly stilted acted scenario, which is clearly meant to represent the 'typi-cal' young man's search for employment. In the twenty-first century, such material would be done cheaply and quickly, and on location. The question is: does this mean that such modern-day 'versions' of these films would be any more revelatory of the particular social phenomena that they set out to examine, simply because they are perceived as 'more authentic' to the modern viewer?[3] The assumption might be that if the use of reconstruction becomes too obvious (either through filmmaker clumsiness or the chang-ing viewing conditions for an older film) then the documentary loses some of its effectiveness.

Same story/different mode: the life, times and death of Aileen Wuornos

Although the examples given above are a mixture of re-enactment, drama-tisation and interviews with real people (or, actors standing in for real people to retain their anonymity), we also need to consider the relationship between different modalities, different ways of telling the 'same' true story. In this respect, the Nick Broomfield documentaries *Aileen Wuornos: The Selling of a Serial Killer* (1992, UK) and *Aileen: Life and Death of a Serial Killer* (2003, UK) stand as an interesting comparison with the dramatised versions of the story seen in the films *Overkill: The Aileen Wuornos Story* (Peter Levin, 1992, US) and *Monster* (Patty Jenkins, 2003, US). For example, the end credits of *Monster* acknowledge the film's 'fictionality' with the following caveat:

> While this film is inspired by real events in the life of Aileen Wuornos, many characters are composites or inventions, and a number of the incidents depicted in this film are fictional. Other than Aileen Wuornos, any similarity to any person, living or dead, is not intended and purely coincidental.

Monster is, on one level, a fictionalised account of (part of) the Aileen Wuornos tale – as this credit makes clear. However, it is not at all clear that anyone knowing the basics of what happened in actuality could mistake the character of 'Selby' (played by Christina Ricci) for anyone other than the real-life Tyria Moore; even though there is some compositing of character traits, and some fictional events included, there is a *residue* of actuality that is unavoidable. Despite the dramatic form that the film takes, it still *refers to* an actuality. This is not to argue that *Monster* is a 'documentary' of course, but in a case such as this, where conflicting versions of the truth are the 'subject matter' as much as anything else, the different modes of telling this story cannot be easily disentangled. The 'whole story' of the Wuornos affair might never be totally told, but its telling lies somewhere in the 'intertext' of court records, documentary films, dramatised films, news broadcasts and so on, rather than any one definitive telling of *the* story. Jerry Kuehl states with some certainty that drama documentaries are completely unable to make any kind of truth claims. His argument appears to rest on a clear and definite split between modes: on the one hand there is 'conventional documentary', while on the other hand there are drama documentaries, which are incontrovertibly 'fictional', due to the fact that they use certain dramatic devices, scripting, actors and so forth. As Kuehl puts it, when referring to what he sees as problems with 'simulated' performances,

> Episodes of which no filmed records exist are ... inaccessible to dramatic artists. The language used by performers may be 'authentic' because derived from court records or other stenographic reports; but the inflections, accent, volume, and pace of what performers utter, as well as their gestures, expression and stance, will not be those of the persons they represent. It's hard to see how the bricks of uniquely insightful portraits can be made from the straw of performances known to be inauthentic before they even begin. This inauthenticity is inescapable. (1988: 107)

As Steven N. Lipkin's (2002) examination of based-on-a-true-story docu-dramas makes clear, however, the questions one needs to ask about these kinds of drama are very much to do with issues of truthfulness, and the viewer's *interpretation* of what they see, to the extent that Kuehl's dichotomy seems hopelessly simplistic. What makes the Wuornos story such an interesting area is that there are a number of different versions of the story, told from different perspectives, and comparing them draws out some of the differences between 'documentary' and 'drama' modalities. Lipkin's work suggests that it is unwise to reject out of hand the possibility that films like *Monster* and *Overkill* can tell us something about the real events to which they dramatically refer. He argues that docudrama versions of events can function as a form of 'persuasive practice', using the legal term of 'warranting' to back up this claim. By warranting Lipkin means the strategies by which docudramatic forms draw together data into an argumentative framework, thereby making an assertion (or set of assertions) about 'what really happened' in a specific, actual scenario:

> Works with a basis in prior, known events, actions and people refer to data already in the public record. They assert moral positions that ultimately become claims made by the film's narrative and warrant these claims through formal strategies that bring together re-creation and actuality. (2002: xi)

Overkill falls into the category of lurid television movie adaptation of a 'true life' story – what Lipkin would categorise as a movie-of-the-week. It is also, unlike *Monster* or either of the Broomfield documentaries, focused a good deal on the police's hunt for Wuornos. In this respect it is a police procedural, which is another staple of the true-life/true-crime types of films. The film begins with the incident where Wuornos (Jean Smart) and Tyria Moore (Park Overall) crash the car they are driving and, fleeing the scene, are spotted by a number of witnesses. It is when this incident is potentially linked to some other crimes that the hunt for the two women leads to the suspicion that Wuornos is responsible for a number of homicides in the area. The warranting process involves the invoking of the facts and figures of the police procedural to 'anchor' the assertions that the film makes, as well as referencing real people and locations, appealing to the audience on its 'based on a true story' foundation.

Due to their obvious documentary status, the Broomfield films do not have to make the same kind of appeals to their audience. There are, however, a range of conflicting 'voices' within the two films. The theatrical trailer for *Aileen: Life and Death of a Serial Killer* is interesting for the way in which it almost completely effaces Broomfield as a presence or 'voice', in stark contrast to the rest of the film. It starts with a white on black caption saying 'A new film by Nick Broomfield'. As we zoom slowly in on a photograph of Wuornos as a young girl, we hear (but do not see) Broomfield: 'Aileen, let me ask you one question. Do you think if you hadn't had to leave your home and sleep in the cars it would've worked out differently?'

Figure 4 *Aileen: Life and Death of a Serial Killer* (2003)

The screen fades to black and then Wuornos appears in extreme close up. She talks about what she might have done, and what her life might have been like, if she had come from a 'right on' family background:

> I would've become, more than likely, an outstanding citizen of America who would've either been an archaeologist, a paramedic, a police officer, a fire department gal, or an undercover worker for DEA, or ar- ... did I say archaeology? ... oh, or a missionary.

As she speaks, the camera holds her in close-up, achieving that 'fly on the wall', observational intimacy that we recognise from many documentaries and is often taken as the marker of authenticity *par excellence*. The brief scene with Wuornos then fades to black and another caption comes up that reads 'Aileen Wuornos was executed for the murder of seven men on 9 October 2002'. This holds for five seconds, before adding 'This is her story'.

It is interesting to note that the word 'true' is absent from that final sentence. *Monster*, the 2003 dramatised account of the Aileen Wuornos story, has the tag-line 'based on a true story'. The different ethical and rhetorical registers we see in films that are 'documentary' and those that are 'fictional' (and there are a number of positions on a spectrum between these two) are blurred somewhat by films that are 'fictionalised' or 'docudrama' renditions of allegedly true events. Also, the 'This is her story' assertion from *Aileen: Life and Death of a Serial Killer*'s trailer attempts to place the 'ownership' of the story firmly in Wuornos's domain. Yet, as Broomfield's films demonstrate – both in the people and events they show, as well as in their very existence – the story was not Wuornos's to tell.

It is certainly ironic that the versions of the Wuornos story that can be termed 'fictional' depend to a large extent on their 'this is a true story' basis. This can of course be explained by the ways in which such tales are often told: they are marketed as a (more or less) truthful rendition of the events as they happened. An obvious difference between *Overkill* and *Monster* on the one hand and the Broomfield documentaries on the other is that the former two tell the story in an 'unfolding' fashion; which is to say, they tell the events as if we are there seeing them happen, from a specific vantage point, and they treat 'what happened' as the main events. The arrest and trial(s) of Wuornos, her subsequent incarceration and execution, not to mention the apparent changing (and some would say, losing) of her mind *en route* are almost completely ignored. This is actually an interesting issue, as it points to the 'self-evident' nature of events as they are presented to us in the fictionalised versions. They are, simply, 'what happened'. Of course, the Broomfield documentaries can only 'document' what happens *after* her arrest (with any 'back story' being filled in via use of Broomfield's voice on the soundtrack, with use of archive photographs and the like). It is in the nature of this kind of documentary that the 'documentariness' resides in how we as viewers are oriented to Broomfield's search for (his own version of) the truth. This is conveyed to us via the apparently 'artless' Broomfield's interaction with Wuornos herself and the people who orbit her world. Broomfield does not use reconstruction or re-enactment of events in order to convey 'what happened'; in many respects, ironically, one could argue that his films show no real interest in 'what happened' but are rooted firmly in the present of the Wuornos case and where it might grotesquely lead next.

A key scene in Broomfield's second film about Wuornos is interesting for the ways that two 'discourses of sobriety' – law and documentary

– clash. It also raises important issues regarding the notion of reconstruction, and how it is often equated to fictionalising. In *Aileen: Life and Death
of a Serial Killer*, Broomfield himself is subpoenaed as a witness in the last
of Wuornos's appeal cases before her execution. He says at the start of
this sequence:

> I like to flatter myself that I was being asked for my legal opinion, but
> it turned out I was there to talk about Steve's [Steve Glazer, Wuornos's
> lawyer] marijuana smoking. The big question was whether Steve had
> consumed seven very strong joints before giving Aileen legal advice
> in prison.

He is then questioned on his techniques in the construction of the so-
called 'Seven Joint Ride' sequence from *Aileen Wuornos: The Selling
of a Serial Killer*. The veracity of what we (think we) see on the screen
(within *Aileen: Life and Death of a Serial Killer*) is called into question by
the prosecutor, who points to the different shirts that Steve is wearing
in contiguous shots. Although Broomfield points out that 'he probably
changed his shirt ... I don't remember' and offers access to the outtakes
from that sequence, it strikes something of a body blow to his integrity as
a documentarist. Certainly, we might as viewers be aware that reconstruction, 'cutting and pasting' and so on, do occur, but this is being held up
as a clear case of something different: deliberately misleading manipulation. Having said this, this is the most important issue with regard to
this sequence – the ways in which the two competing discourses are in a
sense 'battling' for *their* version of 'Wuornos' to hold sway. Wuornos herself is always a highly-mediated presence in the Broomfield films, arguably as 'mediated' (which is to say, kept at some distance from us as viewers) as in either of the fictionalised accounts of her life. In many respects,
both of the Broomfield films are about the wider issues of buying, selling,
wrangling, as well as the betrayals felt and dealt by a highly contradictory
woman. What comes across in these documentaries is that she and her
crimes are a rich seam to be mined for meanings – either wider social
meanings about the death penalty, or killers who happen to be women,
and so on, or what she as a person might 'mean' by any of her statements
(which become increasingly contradictory and problematic as the second
film progresses).

Rights and wrongs

One of the key issues in relation to the Aileen Wuornos story is that she herself had no rights to it. The wrangling over who was going to tell the story is detailed in Broomfield's first documentary, *Aileen Wuornos: The Selling of a Serial Killer*. In this film there are several sequences where Aileen's adoptive mother (Arlene Pralle, a born-again Christian barely older than Wuornos herself) and Wuornos' lawyer, Steve Glazer, wheel and deal for payment for access rights to Wuornos. As Broomfield puts it, as he and Glazer drive up to Pralle's ranch:

> My main problem so far is that Steve and Arlene have told me that Lee [Wuornos] wants $25,000 for the interview. I had always thought that the Son of Sam law prevented people from profiting from their crimes, but apparently the Son of Sam isn't in effect any more.

The next scene then involves Pralle coyly talking about Wuornos, with the occasional aside to Glazer, to check if she should have said something or not. Glazer talks of how 'interesting' and 'fascinating' the story and its characters are, with a view to convincing Broomfield that he should pay the $25,000. The camera pans up to Broomfield, looking sceptical. As he clarifies what the situation is regarding payment, he says (in voiceover): 'In fact, Arlene and Lee's relationship is extremely well-documented, and it seemed far cheaper at this stage to buy in some local TV footage.' The ensuing news report includes footage of both Pralle and Glazer, both maintaining that the only motive for adopting Wuornos is Christian love. This is reiterated by the straight-to-camera comments of the local television news reporter, as she concludes her report.

It is not being argued here that Wuornos should have been able to profit from any films or books that allegedly tell the story of her life or what happened to her and her victims. (Indeed, the law in Florida prohibits this in any case). However, her supposed position as 'America's first female serial killer' turned her into a potent commodity – something that was not overlooked by the adoptive mother and lawyer, nor the Marion County sheriff's department, some of whose officers were alleged to have brokered film and book deals.

As Broomfield notes at one point in *Aileen Wuornos: The Selling of a Serial Killer*:

> All of the press attention had made her into something of a star ... [there were] fifteen studios competing for her story ... two feature films being negotiated ... there were also the chat shows, documentaries, and the books...

The film then cuts to Wuornos, about to be given another death sentence, who rails against this behind-the-scenes dealing in her story:

> The movie *Overkill*, that is a total fictional lie, that they framed me as a first-time ... female serial killer – for the title for that movie ... First female serial killer is not what I am ... and my confessions prove it . . . yet they have taken the confessions and gone 200 per cent against what my confessions stated to get their bogus movie out.

Broomfield then speaks on the soundtrack, as Wuornos continues her statement:

> Lee Wuornos insists she is not a serial killer as she did not stalk her victims or plan her crimes. As with the movie deals, Lee is also surrounded by a web of experts all competing with their own theories on her behaviour. Lee is portrayed as anything from a neglected and abused child who hates her father and is murdering him over and over again, to a sadist who takes pleasure in the agony of her victims.

The next scene sees Broomfield pursuing the sheriff of Marion County at the time, Don Moreland, with a view to questioning him about his and several of his deputies' involvement in the alleged selling of movie rights to the Wuornos story. Moreland runs into a building and locks the door. It is difficult to discern where the truth of the matter lies when so many of the people involved are clearly driven by such mercenary, self-serving motives. However, what this does mean is that the secondary discourses around the Wuornos case – the serialisations, the movie adaptations, the Broomfield documentaries – all must be viewed as part of the 'whole picture'. As discussed above, *Aileen: Life and Death of a Serial Killer* references *Aileen Wuornos: The Selling of a Serial Killer*, when the prosecutor at one of the appeals calls into question Broomfield's documentary methods in that first film. Wuornos herself refers to other mediations of her story, and seems well aware of (at least some of) the implications and worth of her tale. The whole web of film and media references (and here we must include the news broadcasts of the hunt for Wuornos and the subsequent media circus that ensued during her various trials) effectively constitute a bizarre and damning 'supra-documentary', where truth would perhaps be stranger than fiction, if only we could discern where exactly one ended and the other began.

3 THE CHANGING FACE OF THE HISTORICAL DOCUMENTARY

'To articulate the past historically does not mean to recognise it "the way it really was" ... It means to seize hold of a memory as it flashes up at a moment of danger. Historical materialism wishes to retain that image of the past which unexpectedly appears to man singled out by history at a moment of danger. The danger affects both the content of the tradition and its receivers. The same threat hangs over both: that of becoming a tool of the ruling classes. In every era the attempt must be made anew to wrest tradition away from a conformism that is about to overpower it ... Only that historian will have the gift of fanning the spark of hope in the past who is firmly convinced that *even the dead* will not be safe from the enemy if he wins. And this enemy has not ceased to be victorious.'
– Walter Benjamin (1973: 257)

'The only thing new in this world is the history you don't know.'
– Harry S. Truman

In this chapter we shall examine the explicitly *historical* dimension of documentary representation. As already noted in previous chapters the notion of re-presentation, re-construction and the apparent narrativising (some would say fictionalising) impulse inherent in these, is something that raises a number of clear political questions. Who is telling this story? To whom? And why? These deceptively simple questions underpin everything that is important about documentaries and factual programming.

We shall approach this question of documentary representations of history via discussion of films that have used different techniques of 'reconstruction' in how they depict their chosen events. Through the discussion of *The Battle of Orgreave*, *The Peterloo Massacre* (Justin Hardy, 2003, UK) and *The Peasants' Revolt* (Channel 4, 2004, UK), we shall explore how highly-charged historical events are revived, reconstructed and re-enacted for these films. As we shall see, there are different reasons for this in each production, and also different consequences. What they have in common is, as Walter Benjamin intimates, that they 'seize hold of a memory as it flashes up at a moment of danger'. They wish to work through and understand not only 'what happened', but how, why, and what the consequences were for those involved. Furthermore, there is a strong sense in all of these films that there is a need to intervene and redress an imbalance; to tell 'the true story', so to speak. What we therefore get is a kind of polemical 'living history' that falls outside of what most people would commonly, straightforwardly define as 'documentary'. But it is this marginality that gives these films their added political potency. They are 'about' the events depicted, but they are also 'about' the way that those events have been *mis*-represented in the past, how they have been hidden, shunned or covered over.

The technique of reconstructing or re-enacting scenes from history is hardly new, and has been with us since the beginnings of cinema (and arguably before that). There are many examples from the early cinema period where scenes such as the Boxer Rebellion, or famous prize fights were completely re-enacted and then advertised on the basis of their 'authenticity' (see Musser 1990: 200–8, 255–8; Winston 1995: 120). The overriding reason for such 'deception' was of course that cameras were not present at the original events, so if people were to be able to view a 'record' of those events then they would have to be reconstructed. Thus, there is an 'evidential' basis for reconstructing or re-enacting: that is, it is not accurate to assume that the only (or even the main) reason for using reconstruction is for its perceived 'dramatic' impact. This might also be the case, but it is important to remember that reconstruction and re-enactment does also have a more 'serious' and evidential basis, as well as the hard-headed pragmatism of recognising the lack of original record of certain events. Even if there *is* an original record of the events – as is the case with the events that are re-enacted in *The Battle of Orgreave* – there are all sorts of reasons as to why a revisiting of those events, via the processes of re-enactment, can lead to a fuller documenting and understanding of what happened and why.

The Battle of Orgreave and the re-enactment of recent memory

This film stemmed from Mike Figgis's filming of the Jeremy Deller/Artangel project that re-enacted the notorious 'battle' between police and striking miners on 18 June 1984 at the Orgreave coking plant, near Sheffield, at the height of one of the most bitter industrial disputes in British history. The documentary is therefore in part a record of a 'live' event, 'performed' by many people who were involved in the original confrontation, as well as an organised body of well-drilled historical re-enactors. The project was conceived by Deller and Artangel, and carried out with logistical precision by Historical Film Services (part of the EventPlan group). Howard Giles directed the action in real time, and the result was filmed by Figgis for a documentary for Channel 4.[1]

What is interesting here is the status of what we are looking at and listening to. It is not a straightforward 'documentary' by any means. The film itself is a 'record' of the *process* of re-enactment, but the film also explores the very meaning of the term 're-enactment' and the political and emotional resonance that re-enacting those events have for the people involved. The 'realism' of the event makes for quite a bizarre viewing experience: time and again we are shown bone-crunching collisions between 'miners' and 'police'; missiles are thrown, truncheons brandished. These people appear to be really fighting. Yet this is interspersed with on-site interviews with various participants, reflecting on what it means to them to be involved in the re-enactment. This both intensifies and undercuts the 'power' of the battle scenes: undercuts in the sense that it clearly demonstrates that these people *are* performing, playing a role, (re-en)acting; intensifies because there is an active *reflection* on the process of performance itself, how the re-enactment 'measures up' to the actual historical events. *The Battle of Orgreave* is therefore an extremely interesting variation on the 'performative' in documentary. (We shall return below to the notion of the 'performative' documentary and how it is inflected in this film.)

What is at issue when we discuss the very specific type of reconstruction that is re-enactment is, as Bill Nichols makes clear, *proximity*. In other words, how *close* to the real, actual events is the representation? 'Close' in

Figure 5 *The Battle of Orgreave* (2001)

in their evaluations. What we also see and hear, in exchanges that miners have with Figgis while they are waiting in the re-enactment field in lulls in the action during rehearsals, is some very cogent analysis of labour history and the place of the original events within that broad context. For example, one ex-Yorkshire miner, now working in Birmingham, talks about some ex-Nottingham miners who were going to come along and join in the re-enactment:[2]

> [The] Nottingham lads, some of them are where I work, and they were asked to come and do this re-enactment, and I've like just blown up – 'cause it's still in me heart, what happened – and I've said, 'How can you all fucking come and re-enact what was going off when you were back at work at that time, and we had nowt? Not a thing, we were all penniless.'

This prompts another miner in this small group to state the following:

> That's how they've always been; they'll never change ... it's gone on since 1926 this, in General Strike ... they were scabbing in 1926

strike, they scabbed in 1972 strike, they scabbed in 1974 strike, and then 84–85 strike ... as far as I'm concerned in Nottingham – besides them what stopped out – they're just a bunch of scabbing bastards.

As this man turns away, clearly angered, a third miner in the group says over his shoulder, derisively, 'And where's it fucking got 'em?' The injustice these men feel is not just empty bitterness at the betrayal by 'scab' miners, but a clear recognition that their going back to work – and opening up what mining historian and National Union of Mineworkers activist David Douglass calls in the film a 'second front' – led to their own downfall too, as the Thatcher government closed many of the Nottinghamshire collieries as well.

The complexity and contradiction of what happened during this period is embodied by the figure of Mac McLoughlin. Born within sight of the Orgreave plant, McLoughlin was a miner in the 1970s and then served in the armed forces. He then joined the South Yorkshire police force and was on duty on 18 June 1984. His insights are therefore unique and compelling because he talks with authority from both sides of the divide. One thing that comes across from miners who are interviewed as well as McLoughlin is that the animosity was mainly between the striking miners and police officers from outside of South Yorkshire, drafted in to contain the pickets, from London and elsewhere. However, it became clear to McLoughlin that the police (including the local force) 'were being trained up for a specific role', and he talks about the various forms of riot training they were given. He is also brutally frank about what happened during the battle – 'you get pissed off ... it became like a civil war' – but there is one statement that sums up the contradictions he feels and why his interview is as important a part of this documentary as the re-enactment. As McLoughlin puts it: 'One of the reasons I joined the police force were I wanted to [pauses, clearly emotional] – I wanted to do something for community I came from. [Pause] And thanks to Margaret Thatcher, I did – I helped to destroy it.'

Although McLoughlin is not the only person we see interviewed in isolation, the fact that he seems simultaneously so detached from the re-enacted events and yet is such a critically reflective voice on 'what happened', is given added poignancy by the way his interviews are framed. In many respects, he represents the figure of the working-class man, pulled in different directions by historical forces, and yet fully able to articulate his contradictory position.

The Battle of Orgreave is therefore a complex blend of interviews and re-enactment, but the relationship between these two modes – so often taken for granted and not truly reflected upon – is made part of the process of understanding that the film wishes to build. There is also a clear sense that such a reflective mode will lead to a more truthful version of events than was officially sanctioned at the time. An infamous BBC news report edited specific events so that the cause and effect chain was switched. On 18 June 1984, at one point, some police horses charged the miners, causing some miners to throw stones as retaliation. By the time this reached the evening news on BBC1, the film had been edited in such a way as to show the miners throwing stones, thereby (apparently) causing the police to charge them on horses. Tony Benn is interviewed in *The Battle of Orgreave*, remembering that the National Union of Journalists were 'up in arms' as they 'could see quite clearly that the police charge and then the miners threw stones, and [they] were ordered to transpose the order in such a way as to give the opposite impression'. This comment from Benn is followed by a white on black caption that offers an extract from a 'BBC letter of apology' dated 3 July 1991:

> The BBC acknowledged some years ago that it made a mistake over the sequence of events at Orgreave. We accepted without question that it was serious, but emphasised that it was a mistake made in the haste of putting the news together. The end result was that the editor inadvertently reversed the occurrence of the actions of the police and the pickets.

This hardly seems credible, and Tony Benn says as much, when he states 'they didn't make a *mistake* ... whoever gave the orders actually destroyed the truth of what they reported'.[3]

As Tony Benn describes the sequence of events and how they were 'doctored', the film cuts to 'framed' black-and-white moving images with 're-enactment' emblazoned across them in red. The first shot shows a miner throwing a stone, and then there is a 'flash', to signify a slight temporal ellipse, before we see mounted police charging into the assembled miners. There is an interesting use of irony in this sequence. Figgis deliberately draws attention to the 'reconstructed' nature of these shots, and specifically the way in which they are *sequenced*. The elliptical 'flash' is of paramount importance here, as it signifies that something is 'missing': the assumption in most cases would be that what has been cut out is mere 'dead time' (an assumption we have learned from the widespread standard use of ellipses in narrative – fictional and nonfictional – films), but what has been cut is, of course, far more than that. The very process of re-sequencing and re-shaping the material has gone – and the truth has gone with it. Of course, the whole of *The Battle of Orgreave* is based on a (film of a) re-enactment, and the main point of this part of the film is to emphasise the deliberate distortions of 'what happened', so it would fit the agenda of those who wanted the miners to be portrayed as the villains of this particular drama. In effect, Figgis re-enacts the original *fraudulent* sequencing of events (miner throws stone/police charge), but does so in such a way as to undercut what we are seeing.

The authenticity of the re-enactment is held up to scrutiny during the course of the documentary. A number of contributors, including Deller himself, talk about their nervousness and excitement because they are 'uncertain' as to what exactly is going to happen. This is a *re*-enactment, but it is also, crucially, an *enactment*. There are several comments about people taking it too seriously – one of the main police re-enactors says at one point 'some of the extras don't really know when enough's enough'. The film then cuts to a group of miners laughing and joking in front of the camera, and one says (referring to the previous day's rehearsal) 'yesterday – we were playing yesterday, weren't we? Today? Today – it's for real. It's for real ... it's for real...' The dividing line between the re-enacted performance of past events and an actual, real conflict has clearly become very blurred indeed. It is here that the notion of the 'performative' in documentary is very useful.

As discussed in chapter one, Stella Bruzzi defines documentary in general as 'a negotiation between filmmaker and reality and, at heart, a performance' (2000: 154). She further states that those documentaries that can be specifically termed 'performative' are those that acknowledge the dialectical relationship between the real world of actuality and the performed actions of those people who appear in the documentary in question. In other words, the performative is about the *processes* of coming to understand, and often is based on an explicit attempt by the subjects of the film to reflect upon and appraise their situation. There are many moments in *The Battle of Orgreave* where people are quite clearly performing in the sense that they are 'playing a role', but this is complicated by the fact that this may or may not be the 'same' role that they 'played' in actuality in 1984. The self-consciousness that they exhibit on occasion is tempered by some moments of considerable insight into the events of the original Battle of Orgreave and its historical context. In its mobilising of re-enactment (involving many of the original participants), personal reflection and testimony, interwoven with archive photographs and sound (most notably, Thatcher's 'enemy within' speech)[4], *The Battle of Orgreave* becomes an excellent example of folk art. Deller's interest in folk art is clear from previous projects (for example the 'Acid Brass' project)[5] and he is currently collaborating with Alan Kane on the Folk Archive, which looks to collect and curate an ongoing archive of many forms of folk art.[6] As Jennie Syson puts it:

> [Deller] frequently engages in collaborations that seem straightforward, but are actually complex and multi-layered, fusing seemingly disparate elements such as state of the art technology and old-fashioned industry, or contemporary culture and folk art. (2000: n.p.)

Folk art is basically that which is for the people, by the people and will therefore tend to revolve around the very regional, workplace-based, class-driven issues that this film is founded on. Connections can be drawn to the re-enactment societies (some of whom helped with *The Battle of Orgreave*) who 'keep history alive' by re-enacting key battles and other events, as well as traditions of other folk forms such as 'mystery plays'. At the heart of folk art forms is often some notion of performance – this kind of art is often meant to be popular and ephemeral, rather than elitist and durable (with 'durability' translating into direct cash value, as the artwork becomes a commodity). Also central to folk art is the idea of keeping certain stories alive, of ensuring that the 'official' version of events is not the only one to endure. We see this in *The Battle of Orgreave* and its determination to counter the distortions of the Thatcher government and the BBC. We can also see it in slightly different forms in *The Peterloo Massacre* and *The Peasants' Revolt*, to which we now turn.

The Peterloo Massacre and The Peasants' Revolt: even the dead will not be safe...

Appropriately enough, *The Peterloo Massacre* is narrated by a dead man, 22-year-old John Lees, killed in the events of that day. This is a drama-documentary reconstruction of the inquest into his death. But it ends up being much more than that: it becomes a dissection of the infamous events of 16 August 1819 (and their aftermath), and a critique of class relations in nineteenth-century Britain. As part of a series of loosely connected programmes shown on Channel 4 about the 'Georgian Underworld' its remit was to reveal and tell a story that had previously remained hidden. By so doing, it is also revealing of the social and institutional structures that mask and distort specific things. In the same way as we see in *The Battle of Orgreave*, the class struggles inherent in British society are as much the 'subject' of this film as the specific events and characters it portrays. The role of the inquest, we hear, was not to investigate but to cover over the truth (there had already been several inquests that went that way). The dramatised documentary format in this context does not directly revisit and show the viewer a reconstruction of the events that happened in St Peter's Field. Rather, it uses the inquest records and transcripts as a basis for a reconstruction of the *investigation* into what happened. As such, the very nature of the truth of what occurred, the different interpretations of people's actions and the vested interests at the heart of the matter are all held up to intense scrutiny.

In chapter two we referred to Steven Lipkin's discussion of 'docudrama as persuasive practice'. In *The Peterloo Massacre* the emphasis is placed on what Lipkin would call 'warranting' procedures, or the foregrounding of specific data pertaining to the events in an authenticating context. In other words, the references to real people, actual testimony and existing historical locations are all embedded within a compelling dramatic narrative. It is in this combination of actuality and dramatic reconstruction that 'warranting' resides, according to Lipkin. Much of the drama in the film stems from the conflict engendered by class relations of the time: in essence, one 'side' wanted the truth to be told, while the other 'side' wanted it to be covered up. It is from the ebb and flow of that story, the search for the truth as mediated by the conventions of that most compelling of genres, the courtroom drama, that the historical importance of Peterloo eventually emerges. Basically, the film states things that a conventional documentary about Peterloo would not. In the same way as *The Battle of Orgreave* maps out the violence, contradictions, and iconic spectacle of the clash between the miners and police in 1984, *The Peterloo Massacre* takes the recorded statements of those present at the inquest into the death of John Lees, and uses them to prise open some of the hidden aspects of a conventional or received history.

This is why the sixth of Walter Benjamin's Theses on the Philosophy of History, quoted at the beginning of this chapter, is so important in relation to this film in particular. Despite the accurate period details and settings of the film, it is not so much the mapping of the 'way it really was' that is important, as the recognition that histories are constructed – and specific battles won or lost – at what Benjamin calls 'moments of danger'. History is about struggling, seizing, commemorating. And another thing is eminently clear: you need to choose which side you are on. This is not a neutral, 'objective' exercise. One has to believe that 'even the dead will not be safe from the enemy' and act accordingly. *The Peterloo Massacre* does precisely that in the way it uses the story of one man's death to effectively tell the story of a key moment in British history.

It is worth dwelling for a moment on the vexed notion of 'taking sides', as the films discussed in this chapter are prime examples of 'revision-ist' history, where imbalances and biases are addressed in an attempt to 'get to the truth'. The notion of a documentary or factual programme deliberately taking sides is often equated with that film being 'biased' or not having the requisite 'objectivity'. The confusion here is between a sup-posedly 'objective' position that the documentarist takes in relation to their subject, and the idea that this somehow equals 'neutrality' or 'impartiality'. This is flawed on two counts. First of all, there is no such thing as 'an objec-tive position' in the sense that it is often meant; that is, as a position that is somehow magically 'outside' the socio-historical context that it is depict-ing. Secondly, the assumption in all of this appears to be that 'neutrality' should be the necessary aim of all documentarists and, furthermore, that by being perceived to be 'neutral' or 'impartial' (or 'fair and balanced' to borrow the US network Fox News' rather inaccurate slogan) one somehow automatically achieves 'objectivity'.

Mike Wayne usefully makes a distinction between 'objectivity of the object (world)' and 'objectivity of the subject'. The former is a recognition that there exists an 'objective' world, 'out there', independent of human experience. The latter is the erroneous belief that it is possible for particular people (subjects) to take up an 'objective' position, where they can view (and comment upon) things in a manner unencumbered by their 'subjectivity':

> To say that there is a world independent of our experiences of it and practical activities within it is not at all the same thing as arguing that we can be independent of that world, that we can rise above the social interests coursing through our social locations and identifications. (2003: 226)

As he goes on to argue, 'the belief in the possible objectivity of the subject, however, dominates the mainstream media' (ibid.). This certainly comes across in commonsense discourses about documentary and factual programming: the idea that if one shows 'both sides of the argument' that this means that one is being 'fair', because one has made an attempt to remain impartial and objective, an attempt to ignore one's own position or stake in what is being represented. Stuart Hall talks of how notions of impartiality, balance and objectivity lead to a 'false symmetry' in terms of how issues are presented:

> [In broadcasting] all controversial questions *must* have two sides, and the two sides are usually given a rough equality in weight. Responsibility is shared between the parties; each side receives a measure of praise or censure. This symmetry of oppositions is a formal balance: it has little or no relevance to the quite unequal relative weights of the case for each side in the real world. If the workman asserts that he is being poisoned by the effluence from a noxious plant, the chairman must be wheeled in to say that all possible precautions are now being taken. This symmetrical alignment of arguments may ensure the broadcaster's impartiality, but it hardly advances the truth. (1988: 360; emphasis in original)

In other words, to remain stubbornly 'impartial' and 'balanced' in the face of clear *imbalances* in the real world is to actually misrepresent that world, and the power struggles that go on within it.

The narrative of *The Peterloo Massacre* is clearly being related to us from a particular position, one that is seeking to redress the imbalance of the 'official' or 'received' version of events. The narrator, John Lees, becomes the symbol of class tensions that were prevalent in the early part of the nineteenth century. The mass movements calling for fairer representation were unsurprisingly centred on the recent influx of labour to urban areas like Manchester, which was due to the massive expansion seen in the Industrial Revolution. Only a few decades after another revolution, the French Revolution, the signs of ordinary working people organising made certain sectors of society very nervous. This led to a flashpoint on 16 August 1819, when the radical, Henry Hunt, went to speak at St Peter's Field, near Manchester. The Manchester Yeomanry ('shopkeepers dressed up in uniform on horseback, tradesmen with swords' as Lees puts it on the soundtrack) attacked and killed and maimed over six hundred people. As already noted, the film in many respects follows the conventional structure of a courtroom drama, but the basis of what is said is the original transcripts. There is one key exception to this, of course: the voiceover provided by John Lees himself. This acts as an 'editorial' voice, offering ironic commentary on the events and introducing the main players. It transpires during the course of the case that Lees fought at the battle of Waterloo – surviving that day to then be cut down during apparent peacetime. It is also revealed that one of the prominent mill-owners, one of the main groups seeking to cover up the true nature of the events of the day, is actually John Lees' father. Lees makes no secret of the fact that there are conflicts and tensions at play here: James Harmer, the lawyer who ensures that Lees' inquest is not shut down like those before it, is also noted to be trying to 'make a name for himself'. There are of course other typical 'contradictory' characters, such as Robert Hall, who ultimately betrays his class by siding with the magistrates and mill owners, and ends up paying for it. Hall, a cotton salesman, is recruited to tell the 'official version' of what happened – that is, that it was the crowd and not the Yeomanry who sparked the violence. (This inversion of what actually happened in favour of an 'official version' of course mirrors the charging police horses in the events at Orgreave.) Hall's testimony is a disaster, both for him and the people who recruited him. He offers stilted, confused answers and has clearly been coached. At one point, as the coroner adjourns, Hall leans over and says to the lawyer whom we earlier saw recruit him (in one of the few scenes that we might term 'speculative reconstruction'): 'I didn't know whether you wanted me to say it or not.' Lees' voiceover is derisory: 'He *really* did say that! It was in the inquest transcripts. It was published in *The Times*. And he really was *that* bad...' This draws attention not only to the 'warranting' procedures (such as the transcripts, published contemporary sources) and how they are an evidential route into what something was 'really' like, but also crucially emphasises the apparent accuracy of what we are watching – the reconstruction of the inquest itself.

The use of dramatic reconstruction to enable an understanding of historical events is the source of some controversy. This is based on the assumption (discussed in chapter two) that dramatic structure of necessity means that some 'fictionalising' has taken place. However, as Robert Rosenstone points out about *all* historical discourse:

> Omission and condensation ... are integral to all forms of history, written, oral or filmed; for no matter how detailed any portrait of the past, the data included are always only a highly selected and condensed sample of what could be included on a given topic. (1995: 144)

The key is for a documentary representation of historical events not to capture the exact and detailed textures of 'what happened' but rather to communicate the underlying contextual forces at work, and thereby achieve some *explanatory* power rather than simply describing. In *The Peterloo Massacre*, an understanding of the importance of the events in St Peter's Field is not communicated to the viewer by *reconstructing* those events (and thereby providing an 'authentic' or 'pseudo-indexical' rendering of them), but by playing out the underlying ideological conflict that caused the events to happen. Instead of a dramatic rendering of the events of 16 August 1819, the film offers a dissection of the class-based antagonisms underpinning those events, via a dramatisation of the inquest. The massacre itself is merely a symptom of a wider malaise, and it is this that is held up to intensive scrutiny during the course of *The Peterloo Massacre*.

For example, it is made very clear that those that testified 'against' the Manchester Yeomanry at the inquest would have every reason to be in fear of losing their livelihoods (and possibly even their lives).[7] The voiceover tells us as much when introducing William Harrison, a spinner who tells the story of what happened to John Lees. As the deceased Lees says of Harrison: 'He had everything to lose – he was a widower with five kids to feed. But nothing was going to shut him up.' Harrison's testimony is an impassioned and angry indictment of the massacre, drawing a direct comparison with the Battle of Waterloo. This comparison is emphasised by a white-on-black title card, giving Harrison's name and the quote 'At Waterloo it was man to man'; a clear implication that the events at St Peter's Field were, in the words of Harrison, 'downright murder'. At one point in his testimony, Harrison flamboyantly acts out the movements of the mounted swordsmen as they cut people down and the coroner dismissively says 'Oh, you act as well as speak'. Harrison's rebuke is swift: 'Sir, I am no scholar, but I speak the best I can according to truth!' It is clear from the way that the characters are presented and the evidence damningly uncovered that this is a documentary drama that is setting out to redress an imbalance. The dramatic structure and use of nominating title cards gives witnesses such as Harrison the status of 'experts', rather than the deluded troublemakers the 'official' version of events might have us believe.

The official, authenticating voice in many historical documentaries is provided by expository voiceover or the expert, on-screen presenter. Lees' voiceover in *The Peterloo Massacre* subverts the standard expository voiceover with its clear 'stake' in what is being shown to us, and his use of devastating irony. The shortcomings of the standard presenter-led historical documentary are made apparent by *The Peasants' Revolt*. In this programme (an entry in Channel 4's *World's Worst Century* series, about the fourteenth century), Tony Robinson sets out to tell the true story of what happened in the uprising of 1381. There is a clear contrasting with how this story would be told in a conventional history documentary. As Robinson points out:

> The Peasants Revolt wasn't a riot – it was a revolution. Its impact was so shocking that historians from the ruling class deliberately hushed up its true significance. They hid the achievements of ordinary people by scorning them as rioting yokels ... I want to restore the men and women who stood here [in Smithfield] to their rightful place in history.

One of the programme's best strategies is to eschew standard re-enactments or reconstructions. We periodically see people in period costume, and some of the key figures (Thomas Baker, Abel Kerr, John Ball, John Sumner, Wat Tyler) are nominated via captions and the actors who play them are seen in close up. For the most part, however, the use of reconstruction is very limited because the programme-makers are far more interested in locating these events of over six hundred years ago in the contemporary moment. Instead of dramatic reconstruction, the convention of the presenter recounting the events is used, but Robinson is always keen to draw out the 'everydayness' of what might turn out to be momentous events, how they might resonate for a modern-day viewer. For example, as he drives through some council estates in Thamesmead, to the east of modern-day London, and one of the areas where the revolt first gained momentum, Robinson makes an ironic comment about the location not looking like it is 'full of history'. The opening sequence functions in the same way, when the modern-day Smithfield meat market is used as a backdrop for Robinson's comments about how, in 1381, when it was simply a field just outside London, 'it became the stage for one of the most significant events in British history'. When we are told about Thomas Baker organising and leading a deputation to confront a poll tax commissioner at Brentwood, Robinson tells us 'no one knew it at the time, but that was the start of the Peasants' Revolt'. Instead of the 'self-evident' unfolding of history, where important people do important things and ordinary people are precisely that – ordinary, there is a sense here of the contingency of events. As things are unfolding, no one *knows* they are immersed in something that will have an enduring historical importance. The programme therefore draws attention to the way that histories are structured and documented, it reflects upon the historiographical process rather than simply recounting or reconstructing events in a self-evident way. This attention to contextual detail is never clearer than in the sequence where the modes of communication used in 1381 are discussed. As Robinson states, it seems that the southeast of England 'spontaneously combusts' in June 1381. By this he clearly means that this is the *standard* historical explanation for the events – the peasants just started revolting for no apparent reason. What the evidence actually reveals is that the peasants were organised, had a set of objectives and an agenda for social change, and had been pushed into action by a series of inter-related events (higher taxation and its heavy-handed collection being the main focal point). A significant number of them were not even peasants. The way this documentary is structured allows this more complex set of historical forces to come to the fore. In terms of the communication systems used – coded poems, read out in village squares – one contributor draws a comparison between this form of communication d the mass involvement to which it led, and the contemporary use of the internet to spread the word about activist movements and events.

All three of the texts discussed in this chapter seek to engage the viewer in documentary representations of historical events. In the case of *The Battle of Orgreave*, the events in question are in recent memory and there are extant media recordings of them (film, video, photographs). The interesting dilemma addressed by the documentary is how such a re-enactment of politically-charged recent events can actually 'reclaim' the truth of the matter, in the face of distortions on the part of the mainstream media and the state. In the case of *The Peterloo Massacre* and *The Peasants' Revolt*, however, the events are in the more distant past and no direct recording exists (other than court transcripts and newspaper reports for Peterloo and chronicles for the Revolt). For these two films the use of dramatised reconstruction of 'what happened' is a more 'obvious' strategy, but they both manage to use it in ways that move beyond the conventional use and encourage the viewer to reflect on how histories themselves are constructed, dramatised and re-told for future generations.

4   DOCUMENTARY AND COMEDY

In this chapter we shall examine the ways in which modes of comedy figure in documentary and factual films and programmes. This will involve engaging with notions of satire and parody, the role and development of the so-called 'mock-documentary' and the ways in which comedic expression can be seen to be in conflict with notions of documentary truth or objectivity. In many respects, 'comedy' and 'documentary' are similar in the way that they are referred to – wrongly, it may be argued – as 'genres' in commonsense discourse, when in fact they can be better understood as 'modes'. There is not the space here to go into detail about the background of comedy as a mode. The key point is to offer an overview of how documentary strategies (and the intimately related 'current affairs' and 'investigative journalism') are figured in specific films and television programmes, but also to explore how they are inflected and critiqued by modes of comedy. This is a relationship that has yet to receive any sustained attention, but is an increasingly important area of expression.

Defining the field: documentary and satire, irony, parody

One of the first distinctions to make is that between those programmes and films that make their main aim to satirise the textures and conventions of certain types of documentaries and documentary practices, and those that use documentary strategies in order to satirise other subjects. There is of course some overlap between these two categories, but broadly speaking, the former could be termed parodies, as what they are holding up to the satirical light are the formal aspects of specific types of documentary, whilst the latter are more likely to be termed 'satires' proper, because their aim is to critique (via laughter) a wider social structure. Parody has tended to be associated with a ridiculing of the *formal* properties of a genre or individual text. However, it can be argued that such ridiculing of norms and conventions plays a critical, disruptive role and has implications for elements beyond the text itself. This is particularly the case with documentary parodies because documentaries are representing the real social world. Any specific examples of parodic undermining of the assertive, apparently objective stance of documentary inevitably mean that the certainties of documentary as a mode, as a way of understanding and representing the world, are thereby also undermined.

Bill Nichols groups his discussion of the satirical and the ironic in documentary under a subheading: 'The Reflexive Mode of Representation' (1991: 56–75). As he notes, 'The reflexive mode of representation gives emphasis to the encounter between filmmaker and viewer rather than film-maker and subject' (1991: 60). There are a number of types of reflexivity, ranging from the purely formal to the more overtly political. What is being noted here of course is that the range of material that combines documentary and comedy relies on some level of 'reflexivity' on the part of the practitioner and the viewer. Both have to understand and recognise the existing conventions in such a way that it is understood that the result is a parodic or satiric text, rather than an actual documentary. Such reflexivity is suggestive of a 'media literacy' that enables one to be 'in' on the joke, and not fooled. A good example of this is when Carl Plantinga quotes director Rob Reiner with regard to one preview of his film *This is Spinal Tap*: 'A small section of the audience laughed. The rest asked why we would make a serious documentary' about a terrible band they had never heard of' (1998: 320). As Plantinga continues: 'clearly, an appreciation for *This is Spinal Tap* depends on taking it not as a "serious documentary" about an obscure and untalented band, but as a *pseudodocumentary*, a fiction film which ... parodies the forms of documentary' (ibid.).

For documentary and comedy to meet and interact successfully, in the form of parody, there must therefore be a high level of audience 'recognition', of both the original material and the extent to which the parody diverges from it. Dan Harries defines parody in the following terms:

The process of recontextualising a target or source text through the transformation of its textual (and contextual) elements, thus creating a *new* text. This conversion – through the resulting oscillation between similarity to and difference from the target – creates a level of ironic incongruity with an inevitable satiric impulse. (2000: 6; emphasis in original)

Harries then goes on to usefully adapt Rick Altman's (1999) work on film genre in his discussion of film parody. A parodic text can be summed up as one that invokes another highly recognisable text by mimicking it, but at the same time in some very important ways differing from the original. It is this similarity-yet-difference figure that is characteristic of genre as a system, and which explains why genre theory is useful as a way into discussing parody. Harries, following Altman, proposes that every textual system consists of three 'levels': lexicon, syntax and style. The lexicon 'is composed of the elements that populate any film text, such as the setting, the characters, the costumes and the various items comprising the film's iconography, like guns and horses' (2000: 8). Syntax 'is the narrative structure in which the lexical elements reside … in other words [it] is the film's plot' (ibid.). The film's style includes things like camera movements, particular use of sound and so on, and 'weaves itself throughout the lexicon and the syntax to add additional sets of expectations based on that particular type of film text' (ibid.). Harries argues that the parodic emerges from the ways in which a text 'faithfully replicat[es] either the syntax or the lexicon of the target text while altering the other dimension' (2000: 9).

As documentaries are about the real world of actuality, and even those fictional films that parody them must construct a plausible rendering of a believable 'real world' in which the comedy unfolds, then it is straightforward enough to point out that the lexical elements of documentaries (and fictional versions of documentaries such as mock-documentaries) will be recognisable elements from the 'real world', rather than the 'generic' elements of, for instance, a western. Characters that are known to be real people (or who *convince* the viewer that they are real people), recognisable locations, and everyday situations – all of these elements will feature in a documentary or parodic version of one. There are plenty of films that deliberately blur the boundaries between documentary and non-documentary in this regard (indeed, the viewer's understanding of mock-documentaries is entirely based on such a blurring). The successful BBC 'mock-docu-soap' *The Office*, for example, draws its comedy entirely from the creation of a gruesomely plausible workplace, a paper merchants in Slough, and the behaviour of the people who work there. In terms of the lexicon-syntax-style model sketched above, however, it is difficult to discern what is being 'altered' in order for the parody to function. The comedy is subtle to the point of there being no recognisable exaggeration – indeed, there are many docu-soaps that follow exactly the same syntactical patterns (the use of the working day, special events such as the Christmas party, promotions and so on) in order to draw out some of the 'drama' (if that is the correct term) of the everyday. The accuracy of what would be termed the lexical elements in *The Office*, and the way the programme mimics the specific style of this kind of documentary series (observational/fly-on-the-wall camera, occasional straight-to-camera interviews) is note-perfect. Indeed, a programme such as *The Office* highlights the fact that documentary comedies of this kind rely on the viewer to a marked degree. The 'logical absurdity' that is often identified as a marker of parody – a sudden incursion of something that ruptures the verisimilitude and creates incongruity – is absent from

Figure 6 *The Office* (2001; 2003)

The Office; the humour derives from the programme's *sustained* plausibility, rather than the alternation between plausibility and implausibility that is characteristic of parody more usually.[1]

On the other hand, a film such as Mark Lewis's *The Wonderful World of Dogs* (1990, Aus.) appears to inhabit a space that is somewhere between a 'proper' documentary and a spoof. Like his earlier film, *Cane Toads* (1988, Aus.), does for its eponymous species, the film offers statistics and information about dogs and their living habits, and is clearly about the real world in that sense. Where it veers into a grey area in definitional terms is when its interviews and reconstructions take on an obvious comedic edge. For example, one sequence begins with a tiny Chihuahua sheepishly wagging its tail as it swipes the burger from a huge burger bun. Cut to the dog sitting on his mistress's lap as she recounts the tale of how the Chihuahua was spirited away in the bill of a pelican, while she was walking the dog by the sea one day. At this point the film moves into an obvious flashback mode – slightly blurred edges to the frame, echo on the voiceover – with the clear indication that this is in fact the burger-swiping Chihuahua's dream. The reconstruction is 'camped up' for all it is worth – complete with overacting and one memorable shot of the tiny dog aloft in a ridiculously-faked pelican bill. The 'dream' ends when the pelican drops the dog and he awakens with a relieved gulp. Lewis's films tend to use such techniques quite frequently and are often dismissed as 'not documentary' as a consequence. However, we have no reason to believe that the story itself, although seemingly ludicrous, is not true. All Lewis is doing then is 'reconstructing' an event – hardly something that, in and of itself, renders the film a 'non-documentary'. Certainly, its deliberately staged nature makes the viewer think about the status of what they are watching, but in this respect it is simply using comedy as a 'reflexive' strategy, as Nichols (see above) has noted.

What some viewers find problematic about documentary films like *The Wonderful World of Dogs*, *Cane Toads*, or some of the work of Errol Morris (for example, *Gates of Heaven* (1978, US)) is the sense that we are being shown *faked* interviews, actors *pretending* to be bizarre eccentrics, and that the joke is somehow on the viewer. However, most mock-documentaries are easily discernible as such and can be enjoyed accordingly. There are some infamous cases – for example, the New Zealand reception of *Forgotten Silver* (Costa Botes and Peter Jackson, 1995, NZ), as documented by Jane Roscoe and Craig Hight (2001: 146–50) – where some viewers 'fall into the trap' (as they see it afterwards) of believing the parody is an actual documentary. An intriguing alternative to this is the reception of a film like *American Movie: The Making of Northwestern* (Chris Smith, 1999, US), about an actual person trying to make a real low-budget film, which was taken in some circles as an elaborate parody of a particular kind of documentary, and talked about by some as if it was a mock-documentary.[2]

The mock-documentary, or mockumentary, is one of the more prevalent forms of comedy documentary. Although not all mock-documentaries are necessarily comedies (or comedies of the same type[3]), the comedic mock-documentary certainly predominates. Roscoe and Hight have produced the most sustained analysis of mock-documentary to date. Theirs is a useful work because it constructs a tentative typology of mock-documentary, locates the form in relation to notions of 'factuality' in documentary and argues that the (fictional) mock-documentary form is essentially a 'subversion' of a specific 'normative' way of looking at and understanding the world. They also argue that the mock-documentary constructs a particular (and active) position for the viewer, due to the 'ambivalence and ambiguity' of the mock-documentary as a parodic text: 'Parodic texts talk to a knowing viewer. The comic elements of parody can be appreciated only if we recognise the object being mocked. The mock-documentary can develop the complexity inherent to parody only if we are familiar with the codes and conventions of documentary, and its serious intent' (2001: 31). The flip side of this observation is that there will be inevitable occasions where viewers will effectively 'misrecognise' a 'proper' documentary as a mock-documentary, simply because of the tone used, or the presence of bizarre characters. Some viewers will read these elements and strategies as part of the comedic repertoire and draw the conclusion that the film is a mock-documentary. The problem with this is that mock-documentaries are by definition *fictional*, albeit a fiction that comments astutely on *documentary* filmmaking and its assumptions. What we have with such films as *Cane Toads* and *The Wonderful World of Dogs* are examples of nonfictional films that use exaggerated techniques for comic effect. It should be noted that many mock-documentaries adopt 'observational' or 'fly on the wall' strategies as their shorthand for 'documentariness'; documentaries such as those made by Mark Lewis use more 'obvious' comedy strategies to draw attention to (and 'mock') the assumptions and objectives of documentary as a whole.

A discourse of (in)sobriety? Parodies of documentary as a source of knowledge

There are a range of films and television programmes that have as their basis a humorous and ironic stance on the ability of certain types of documentary output to inform us. For instance, there are programmes that use comedy to offer some critical distance on the certainties offered by many conventional representations of history (see also chapter three's discussion of representations of history). Similarly, there are parodies of educational and informational programming, such as the note-perfect spoof of early 1980s-era schools science programmes, *Look Around You* (BBC, 2002, UK) Finally, there are comedy programmes that draw upon some of the conventions of lectures and the imparting of knowledge and as such can be said to be satirising the commonsense belief in voices of authority and discourses of sobriety.

Ultimately, what any spoofs of specific modes of nonfiction/information films tell us is that the originals have achieved some level of recognisable or 'canonical' status. This must happen for them to function as parodies. For example, the 'Mr Cholmondeley-Warner' sequences from the Harry Enfield comedy sketch shows (for example, *Harry Enfield and Chums*, *Harry Enfield's Television Programme*) – short informational sequences in a 1930s/1940s 'Griersonian' style, where well-dressed men engage in stilted exchanges in order to elucidate and inform on a particular issue. These are parodies of a specific style of nonfiction filmmaking, but offer satirical comment on outdated social mores ('Women: Know Your Place!' and so on). A strong component in these short films, *Look Around You*, and any other films or programmes that engage in this kind of commentary on modes of documentary, is the mobilising of a *nostalgic* frame. As well as the invoking of the original that we see in any parody, there is a double edge to the humour: viewers are meant to revel in the ways in which the parody *resembles* the original, but they are also meant to thereby find the original funny and, especially, how the parody diverges from it *whilst* resembling it. In the case of the Mr Cholmondeley-Warner sketches, the rather clumsy, artless style is amusing, but it is really the expository 'certainty' of what are actually class- and gender-based assumptions and prejudices that is being satirised. This is what raises such material above the level of simple pastiche.

As both Harries and Roscoe and Hight point out, the parodic can be seen as a stage in the life cycle of a genre (as outlined in John G. Cawelti's essay (1985) on *Chinatown* (Roman Polanski, 1974, US)). The conventions of a particular type of filmmaking become so familiar to viewers that they are literally 'laughable' as clichés. But it is vital that a level of 'recontextualisation' occurs for these conventions to register as funny. Such recontextualisation can occur in a number of ways though. In the case of *Look Around You* and the Mr Cholmondeley-Warner material, the sober discourse of an informational documentary mode is juxtaposed with ludicrous statistics and outright lies, so that the original conventions appear ludicrous too. A crucial thing to note is that the viewing context can contribute to this parodic shift, so that a film such as *Reefer Madness* (Louis J. Gasnier, 1936, US) is viewed in a modern context for its camp value and hysteria over drug use. A didactic cartoon such as the patriotic *Old Glory* (Chuck Jones, 1939, US), which includes some simplistically tub-thumping notions of US history, was screened between acts at the Filmore Stadium in San Francisco in the late 1960s, and was appreciated by the audiences for its 'countercultural' worth, especially the cartoon's ending where Porky Pig is seen enthusiastically saluting the US flag (see Schneider 1994). What such examples prove is that the audience plays an important part in defining the 'place' of specific films. Harries discusses the ways in which parody in some sense overturns or challenges the idea of a 'canon' (in that parody ridicules well-established forms), but he also astutely points out that parody films can be read in a 'canonical' way by audiences, and that they can constitute their own orthodoxy.

A good example of the fusion of elements of stand-up comedy and the often sober discourse of documentary is the series *The Mark Steel Lectures* (BBC, 2003–2004, UK). In chapter three we examined the ways in which documentary representations of historical events need to be seen as more complex than is commonly supposed, especially with regard to the issue of reconstruction and re-enactment. *The Mark Steel Lectures* (originally a BBC Radio 4 series, then transferred over to BBC Television) takes the biographical documentary model of various famous individuals and plays it for laughs. But the point is not just to demonstrate that characters like Karl Marx or Ludwig van Beethoven had 'more to them' than their legacy often lets on, but to deconstruct using humour the very notion of a certain type of documentary discourse. As Steel demonstrates, the conventional historical biography documentary tends to be a narrowly-conceived affair, discussing 'great figures' for certain aspects of their legacy, but omitting much of the historical context in which this legacy was created and thereby missing why it should have any relevance to many people in the contemporary moment. A case in point is Beethoven. Clearly, any documentary about Beethoven should talk about the music he created, but Steel locates what the man did in the context of the cultural and class conflicts of the late eighteenth and early nineteenth centuries, and makes an impassioned case for why Beethoven should be seen as not only a hugely gifted composer, but as the radical force that he actually was. The comedy here is a critique of the ways in which Beethoven (and classical music in general) has his 'rough edges' smoothed so that he and his work are made more palatable for middle-class consumption. What is lost are the very things that connect someone like Beethoven to a large range of people; people who would no doubt perceive classical music as being 'not for them'. In the programme there are several hilarious moments where Steel outlines the contradictory status of someone like Beethoven. From a modern perspective, with the benefit of hindsight, he is a composer-genius; yet in order to live in his era, he had to initially rely on the patronage of royalty (who treated composers as gifted as Beethoven and Mozart as little more than performing seals, to add to their social standing) and, later, by teaching music to the children of the noble class. Steel points out the contempt that Beethoven had for this kind of work. As he speaks on the voiceover, we see a student playing the piano while Beethoven wanders around in pyjamas, listening to a personal stereo, obviously completely uninterested. Another of these 'reconstructions' shows someone with a passing 'look-alike' resemblance to Elton John, smugly playing 'A Song for Guy' as Beethoven rolls his eyes in boredom behind him. Earlier in the programme, as Steel makes a case for Beethoven's musical and cultural importance, the camera pans along a row of faked record sleeves, each spoofing a famous musical icon: Beethoven-as-Eminem, Beethoven-as-Johnny Cash, Beethoven-as-Bob Marley. (Later in the programme, Beethoven even appears as one of the Ramones.) As a passionate, radical, gifted voice during the turbulent times immediately after the French Revolution, Beethoven can only be fully understood in these 'popular' terms. Steel's comedic take on the standard documentary therefore not only gives more of the historical context of Beethoven's time, but also shows the things that make him still relevant today: it is in the contrasting of historical figure (and the facts about their life) with such apparently incongruous modern-day elements that the true complexity of the individual and the historical forces that shaped him emerge.

Clearly, then, these films are parodies of a certain type of educational historical biography genre. They include many patently silly skits, such as a young boy in a seventeenth-century wig, pretending to be Isaac Newton, or an actor, playing Karl Marx, standing ignored in a modern-day street as he proffers leaflets about world revolution – the one time that someone pauses in front of him being to ask directions. But in parodying the *form*, the intention is to satirise the broader (mis)understanding of how history is constructed, and the role of specific people within it. As noted above, if the objective of the programmes were simply to fill in some of the things that are usually omitted when making programmes about these people, then they would be of less interest than is being proposed here. The films are not simply showing the quirks and foibles of people like Thomas Paine, Sylvia Pankhurst or Leonardo da Vinci. By virtue of parodying some of the conventions of the standard biographical programmes, Steel provides a satirical take on the epistemological rationale of such programmes. This irreverent approach to the received wisdom of certain ways of understanding the world offers an important route out of certain 'dead-ends' of history, where the 'standard' mode of explanation is inadequate, precisely because it effaces the very things that make things happen in history – ordinary (and sometimes extraordinary) people and their struggles. As we saw in chapter three, the standard or official explanation of what happened at Orgreave is riddled with distortions and inconsistencies, because it is an explanation that tries to minimise the real reasons for the showdown that day. Likewise, the events shown in *The Peasants' Revolt* are commonly 'explained' as a sudden, inexplicable uprising, fuelled by outside agitators, rather than an organised revolution against unjust laws. The approach to documenting history seen in these programmes and *The Mark Steel Lectures* is one that uses alternative explanations and considerable humour to subvert the pomposity of the traditional, received wisdom.

'Investigative comedy': current affairs and journalistic models

Mockumentaries aside, a commonsense assumption seems to be that the modes 'comedy' and 'documentary' do not mix easily, and one needs to be very careful when walking the line between them. This is particularly the case with satirical current affairs programming and other examples where the dominant models of professional journalism are critiqued in some fashion. Jon Plowman points to this dichotomy:

> If you've got something to say of a serious nature that adds to the political debate, the place to say it is *Newsnight*, or in a documentary form. If you've got something to say that's funny, the place to say it is a comedy programme. And the problem is the marriage of the two. (Quoted in Keighron 1998: 129)

What seems to be at issue is the contradiction inherent in trying to combine the supposedly 'objective' discourse of documentary and current affairs with the notoriously 'subjective' nature of comedy. What is funny, it seems, is all a 'matter of taste' (or opinion), whereas the empirical certainties we have learned to expect from a documentary text are precisely that – clear, measurable and anything but a matter of opinion.

Yet this is based on a doubly false premise: the related ideas that first of all, documentary discourse exists on a plane where facts are presented 'impartially', and in a 'balanced' manner, in order to reach external truths; and, secondly, that comedy discourse is somehow unable to access such truths, and can only render the comedian's own view on the issue. This is flawed quite simply because many documentaries are of a polemical nature, and advance a specific and identifiable argument. Even those that appear 'more objective' are functioning within a set of conventions and institutional contexts that mean they will draw upon certain ways of doing things, and their apparent balance and impartiality are often due to the effacement of a distinct 'voice' in favour of notions of 'professionalism' (a very important term for journalists). In other words, what we have here are two inter-related myths. A documentary could be one-sided and opinionated (while masquerading as balanced and objective), and actually reveal nothing (new) about the world; a comedy programme could advance a convincing argument about certain issues in the world, while remaining fundamentally a comedy programme. This is, after all, what we should view documentary as – a text that advances an argument, marshals evidence, or makes assertions and reaches conclusions *about issues in the real historical world*. It is just as possible to do this in a comedic mode or idiom as it is a serious and 'sober' one. As programmes such as *The Day Today* (BBC series, 1994, UK) and *Brass Eye* (Channel 4, 1997/2001, UK) demonstrate, with their satirical mimicking of the conventions of television news reporting and current affairs, it is entirely possible to produce a programme that is both ludicrous and deadly serious. For instance, the episode of *Brass Eye* that 'investigated' the drug 'Cake' was castigated for joking about so serious an issue.[4] This misses the point, as what is being satirised is a vital issue in relation to documentary: the fact that we live in a world where there is a super-abundance of information available to us, but that actually very little of this information is presented in a way that encourages analysis, reflection and intellection. Instead, things are presented as self-evident truths (for example, drugs are bad). *Brass Eye* takes that oversimplification to some sort of logical conclusion. What it 'documents' is simply that the level of debate on a number of serious issues is severely distorted by reliance on emotive and moralising standpoints (represented here by the eager celebrities queuing up to condemn the drug). As such, I would suggest that *Brass Eye* is actually a far more serious (and necessary) programme than even most of the people who praised it would allow. It does not just mock these people by pointing to their gullibility, but it asks us to see their gullibility as part of a broader context, a context that is informed and structured by the codes and conventions of contemporary current affairs programming, as well as an increased obsession with 'celebrity' culture (an issue is not important unless it has a 'celebrity' endorsement).

The tension noted earlier – between wanting to be taken seriously and wanting to be funny – is something that rears its head in relation to the work of Mark Thomas. A stand-up comedian, always politically committed, he has more recently moved towards the world of political activism and direct action. His programme for Channel 4 began life as *The Mark Thomas Comedy Product* in 1996 but was soon renamed as *The Mark Thomas Product* to perhaps underline the greater emphasis on investigative journalism rather than comedy. However, the show remains a potent combination of stand-up routines, on-location interviews and pranks and a clear, committed transmission of information on a topic; it is an interesting hybrid of detailed reportage and satire – in effect, a form of documentary 'investigative comedy'. What we eventually decide to call such a programme ('investigative comedy'? 'documentary stand-up'?) matters less for the moment than recognising that there is no logical reason to set up and maintain a 'dividing line' between the 'discourse' of comedy and the 'discourse' of documentary. It is possible for a programme to 'do' both. Indeed, the comedy of such a programme is firmly rooted in a recognition by the audience that things that were previously swept under the carpet are being brought out into the open, much to the discomfort of politicians, arms dealers and unscrupulous businesspeople. The programmes set out to reveal previously hidden issues and situations, they gather and present evidence, advancing an argument about the real social-historical world, they have a recognisably didactic/argumentative voice running through-out – all of these are characteristics of certain types of documentary. The techniques used link Thomas's work to other satirical activists, such as Michael Moore in the US, whose *TV Nation* (1994–95, US) programme (and his subsequent film work) featured similar scenarios, where Moore would confront perpetrators of social injustice.

Although Thomas has by now become well-known to the people he challenges, there is still a sense that he uses their own discourses against them. Far from the strident, megaphone-toting activist, Thomas often uses careful and detailed research, and a quiet yet insistent tone when questioning people. He often appears in such sequences wearing a suit and tie, playing the part of the respectable (and respectful) interviewer. Purposeful disruption is never far away, though. In one 1998 episode of the series, Thomas and some supporters ran amok at the Harrods sale, ruining the dramatic '10, 9, 8...' countdown to the opening of the doors, and generally making a nuisance of themselves. This framed an investigative piece about Harrods owner Mohammed El-Fayed's questionable record as an employer. One of Thomas's most effective campaigns was an investigation into the Conditionally Exempt Works of Art scheme (CEWA). In exchange for 'defer-ral' of the Inheritance Tax on certain artworks, land or buildings (worth 40 per cent of the item's value), people who have inherited notable items have to maintain them and allow the general public 'reasonable access'. Thomas revealed that many rich people were using this as a tax dodge, a loophole where they avoided paying the 40 per cent tax, but then kept the item as if it were their own 'private' property. The terms and conditions of the CEWA scheme mean that the item in question is not 'private' property in the com-monsense meaning of that term, as ordinary people can view the item. The programme not only outlined this previously well-hidden state of affairs but was instrumental in starting a campaign of direct action, to encourage as many people as possible to force inheritors to make items available for viewing. In many cases, the owners simply paid the tax that was due and removed the item from the CEWA list, rather than have to comply with the rules on public access. This particular segment was typical of many in the Mark Thomas programmes: offering a detailed exposition of a scandalous misuse of taxpayers' money; outlining in some detail (during the stand-up routines) the figures involved; then showing evidence of what can be done to change this situation for the better. As well as being very funny, and demonstrating Thomas' highly accomplished live comedy technique, the programme is a sharp campaigning documentary, using the discourses of grass-roots activism and direct action to show that ordinary people can make a difference.

Another example of the mixing of comedy and documentary modes is *Osama and Us* (Jamie Campbell and Joel Wilson, 2003, UK). *Osama and Us* was clearly inspired by the irreverent 'door-stepping' techniques of Michael Moore and Mark Thomas (see, specifically, his *Mark Thomas: Weapons Inspector* (Channel 4, 2003, UK)), as well as the absurd and surreal immersion in the language of news-speak that we see in the work of Chris Morris (*Brass Eye* in particular). The film is on one level a parody of certain models of investigative journalism: the two journalists (Campbell and Wilson) take as their cue the $25 million reward that was offered by the US for the capture of Osama Bin Laden, and they travel around seeking clues as to where he might be, speaking with people who have associated with him. If this was all they did then the film would be of limited interest. However, the intention of this documentary is to reveal the absurdity of some of the claims of President Bush and Prime Minister Blair and their allies, by taking these claims completely at face value and pursuing them to their logical conclusion. At various points in the film the main investigator muses that perhaps the US were not that interested in finding bin Laden. The satirical suggestion is that, despite their statements to the contrary, it is very much in the allies' interests to keep bin Laden 'out there' as a bogeyman, capable of anything. At one point, the investigator joins a melee of reporters at an airport, to meet Hans Blix, just arrived back from Baghdad. Wishing to discover whether bin Laden was in Iraq, the investigator calls out 'I just wanted to rule it out: he wasn't there?' Blix's reply is 'I saw the Iraqi government...' Once he hears this, the investigator says 'OK, thanks for that'. Giving a businesslike nod and perusing a piece of paper, he walks off, then looks straight into the camera and says 'He's not in Iraq.' The clear suggestion here is that an off-the-cuff remark or soundbite can be taken at face value, particularly if it fits with an already-sanctioned view of things (and especially if it comes from a recognised 'expert'). Blix says one thing; the reporter takes it to mean something else. The satiric intention here is to highlight the way that many reporters can have a fixed agenda, but also to suggest that the authorities actually expended limited effort to find bin Laden, as he was more use to them as a fugitive. No evidence of something leads inexorably to an emphatic, certain answer. The reporter's 'investigation' as to bin Laden's whereabouts therefore satirically critiques the self-serving investigations carried out by the US and her allies.

From the simplest of spoofs of certain types of information films, to parodies and satires that ironically critique the apparent objectivity and certainty of documentary as a cultural practice, the inter-relationship between modes of documentary and comedy is as extraordinarily complex as it is rich and diverse. Central to this area's importance is the role assigned to the viewer: the ability to recognise and interpret material that is mimicking, mocking and faking for all manner of reasons. The mock-documentary is currently the prevalent form of documentary-comedy, and raises all sorts of questions about authenticity, plausibility and audience belief. However, there have been some interesting recent developments: hybrids of comedy and the serious discourses of investigative journalism and activism; and comedic critique of conventional historical accounts of events. What these developments demonstrate is that documentary need not be shackled to the notion of a 'discourse of sobriety', nor does documentary-comedy have to mean spoofs or mock-documentaries alone.

5   ANIMATION AND DOCUMENTARY REPRESENTATION

The focus of this chapter is the relationship between documentary and animation. There is a long tradition of animation being used as a mode of expression *within* documentary – for example to demonstrate the complicated workings of machinery in an otherwise live-action documentary about industry. We could more accurately refer to these sorts of films as documentaries with animated sequences. However, the point here is not merely to outline how documentaries might *use* animation, but to investigate some of the interesting problems that arise when examining where these two apparently discrete modes meet in a more direct manner. In other words, we shall explore actual 'animated documentaries'. In chapter four we looked at documentary and comedy as modes, and the intention is to do the same thing here in relation to animation and documentary. The contention is that there is a tendency to view documentary as a mode of discourse that will not allow such subjective, expressive aspects as we associate with comedy and animation. This tendency is strongly rooted in the philosophical basis of certain forms of representation – and therefore means we must think through some complex debates about realism and representations of the real – but here it will be argued that it is errone-ous and unhelpful if we wish to fully understand how documentary and animation (and comedy, for that matter) actually work. As we have seen in earlier chapters, 'documentary' must now be seen as a range of strategies in a variety of media; we can no longer cling to essentialist notions of what the term might mean. As previous chapters have outlined, there is a useful distinction to be drawn between the categories 'nonfiction' and 'documentary', and the purpose in this chapter is to examine the ways in which this distinction is inflected by another interesting category of moving image production – animation. The notion that a documentary can only deal in an apparently straightforwardly 'realist' set of representations has therefore come under challenge in recent times, and engaging with animated documentary demonstrates clearly how documentary can be the realm of subjectivity, fantasy, and non-normative approaches to understanding the world around us.

Animation has long been used in informational and educational films that can clearly be included as part of the documentary category. During the First World War, there were the *Kineto War Map* (F. Percy Smith, 1914–16, UK) series of films that used animated map sequences to show the progress of the war. Indeed, there was a strong association in this period between animated films and propaganda (see Ward 2003; 2005a). A later use of animated documentary in a propaganda context was Disney's *Victory Through Air Power* (Clyde Geronimi, Jack Kinney, James Alger and H. C. Potter, 1943, US), a combination of animation and live action. Animation was also used in the documentary context by Len Lye, a New Zealand-born innovator who worked under John Grierson at the Empire Marketing Board and GPO Film Unit. Lye's films used techniques such as 'direct animation' (scratching or painting directly onto the film strip) and their often abstract patterns and shifting rhythms are a clear link to a more modernist, experimental tradition of filmmaking. At the same time, a film such as *Trade Tattoo* (1937, UK) can clearly be read as a documentary: in the film, Lye uses found footage from other GPO documentary films showing aspects of trade and industry. These were then 'creatively interpreted' via colour optical printing and other techniques; Lye also added some abstract patterns and playful captions over some of the original footage, as well as an up-tempo soundtrack. The result is a kinetic paean to the hustle and bustle of trade, where the animation techniques used literally seem to 'bring to life' this apparently everyday activity.

As well as such animated films (which are often discussed within the category of experimental or avant-garde film, rather than documentary; see O'Pray 2003: 44–7), the other main area where animation has addressed social issues in a way that compels us to consider the relationship with documentary is in what might broadly be termed the 'independent' sector, especially that populated by women practitioners. There is a long association between animation and female expression (see Pilling 1992), and the work of Candy Guard, Joanna Quinn, Caroline Leaf, Ruth Lingford and others – while not necessarily 'documentary' animation – certainly uses animation and its specific mode of representation to address real social issues. One body of work that does successfully combine documentary and animation in order to make a political statement about the world is the work of the Leeds Animation Workshop. The Workshop was formed on an informal basis in 1976 in Leeds, England, when some women came together to address the lack of workplace childcare facilities in their area by making an animated film, the campaigning *Who Needs Nurseries? We Do!* (1976, UK). The group subsequently continued to use animation as a way to address social issues, making films that offered a polemical, femi- nist-oriented perspective on representation (for example, *Give Us a Smile* (1983, UK)). The work of the Leeds Animation Workshop therefore is a good example of a specific mode of practice – that of the community-based, 'activist' producers. As Irene Kotlarz points out, the films were 'intended to provoke discussion rather than simply to entertain' (1990: 240). The fact that the workshop more often than not produced animated documentaries points to the perception of animation as a mode that can draw together complex social issues and simplify matters (sometimes to ironic effect) to present an argument about the real social world. *Who Needs Nurseries? We Do!* for instance, speaks from the children's point of view – a strategy that intensifies this feeling of the problems actually being simple and straight- forward (and in urgent need of a solution).

Typologies and categorisations

As we saw in chapter one, the way in which we categorise documentaries is very important. Maureen Furniss (1998) has suggested that all moving image productions should be conceptualised as existing on a continuum characterised by the poles 'mimesis' and 'abstraction' and this certainly allows one to think about the *relative* weight given to different modes of representation within any particular motion picture. Animation – and animated documentary in particular – 'suffers' from the predisposition to equate notions of realism with an *indexical correspondence* to a pro-filmic actuality. In other words, for something to 'be realistic' it is commonly supposed that it must directly *resemble* the thing that it represents. In the case of documentary especially, we tend to find that this translates into the idea that documentary as a category not only has to look and sound a certain way, but that any form of 'subjectivity' or 'personal expression' is out of place. As we have seen in earlier chapters, though, there is a long tradition of 'creativity' (or 'creative treatment' to use a Griersonian phrasing) in documentary production. Animation represents one of the clearest challenges to simplistic models of what documentary is and can be, quite simply because you cannot have an animated film that is anything less than completely 'created'. The frame-by-frame production process means that animation is the most 'interventionist' of modes; and, some would argue, this level of intervention (allied with, as we shall see, often startling levels of 'expressivity' and experimentation) means that it cannot adequately represent the real – which should be one of the defining features of documentary. Yet, as we shall see, animation is a mode perfectly suited to documentary production.

Paul Wells has offered a useful typology of animated documentary modes. He refers to the 'documentary tendency' of some forms of animation and sketches four modes – the imitative, the subjective, the fantastic and the postmodern. The 'imitative' mode is that type of animated film that offers an imitation (or pastiche) of live-action documentary tropes. Key examples here are some of Disney's instructional shorts (for example, the *You and Your...* series (1955–57, US)) or Winsor McCay's *The Sinking of the Lusitania* (1918, US), which at times startlingly resembles a live-action newsreel. All of these animations in some way borrow recognisably documentary conventions. As Wells points out:

> The closer that animated films conform to 'naturalist' representation and use the generic conventions of some documentary forms (for example, the use of 'voiceover'; the rhetoric of 'experts'; the use of 'factual' information etc), the more it may be said to demonstrate documentary tendencies. (1997: 41)

A good recent example of this kind of documentary is *What's Blood Got To Do With It?* (Andy Glynne, 2004, UK), one of a series of short animated documentaries.[1] The film is a parody of the public information film tradition, using expository techniques to put across a highly compressed history of blood and blood donation. In this respect it can be seen as a 'consciousness-raising' film, asking people to not only understand the issues, but to also take some positive action and give blood. The voiceover (by comedian Alexei Sayle) and the images are deliberately comical, playing on the cartoonal style of certain types of animation. (Compare this to another film in the series, *Leona. Alone* (Rani Khanna, 2004, UK) about a girl who suffers from sickle-cell disease, where the animation style is less frenetic and the film uses the girl's own voiceover as the soundtrack – this is more akin to what Wells calls the 'subjective' mode (see below)). Indeed, many of the jokes appear to draw attention to the 'condensation' that is occurring: in order to fit this much information into the three-minute running time, the pace and connections between different aspects of the information require that a lot is condensed, leading to some amusing juxtapositions. For instance, the condensation of large eras of history – and their differing views of what blood is, what it does, and so forth – is very amusingly achieved via some spoof magazine covers, where the images and captions speak volumes about how scientific progress rapidly changed how blood was viewed. Although there is a fairly typical (animated) use of caricature and comical condensation, therefore, we should also note that this is in the service of an expository documentary impulse – in other words, the straightforward presentation of 'self-evident' facts and information about the subject matter. While there seems to be some licence taken with how the animation is presenting the material, it is actually the case that this film follows many of the conventions of standard expository documentaries.

The subjective mode is one that accentuates what some would say is the inherent 'subjectivity' of animation: much animation emphasises the specific interventions of the animator – their 'worldview' for want of a better term – and animated documentaries that fall into this category play upon this by linking the creative acts of the animator with apparent access to the subjective thoughts of their main characters (real people). Subjective documentary often 'moves beyond its basis as the expression of an individual voice and finds correspondence in viewers to the extent that it articulates social criticism' (1997: 43). The animatedness of such documentaries is something that draws out some of the problematic issues of a belief in an 'objective' position from which certain stories can be told.[2] Below are some notable examples that arguably come into this category.

The fantastic mode of animated documentaries in this typology is one that explores what lies beneath the surface of 'everyday' reality, often with a surrealist approach as typified by someone like Jan Svankmajer. As Svankmajer contends, he looks to make 'fantastic documentaries' using what he terms 'militant surrealism'. The suggestion is that 'objective reality is an illusory, unhelpful and ultimately misleading concept' (1997: 44). As Wells points out, although this mode can be seen as an extension of the subjective mode, it can tend towards the abstract and surreal, so that rather than the films transmitting a self-evident 'look' into a specific person's subjective view of their situation (as is the case with, say, *Leona. Alone*), what is achieved is often oblique, mysterious and contradictory. Of course, it is entirely possible for a 'subjective' film to exhibit these characteristics – especially so if the subject in question has some 'problem' with communicating their own subjectivity (see below for the discussion of *A is for Autism* (Tim Webb, 1992, UK)) – which is why Wells makes the point about these categories overlapping to some extent. However, it is certainly the case that one of the most widespread and compelling forms of animated documentary, especially in recent years, has been the 'creative interpretation', via animated visuals, of a real person's testimony or reminiscence.

If the 'fantastic' mode offers a glimpse beneath the surface of the everyday, and raises doubts about documentary's ability to adequately represent the fullness of existence, then Wells' final mode, the 'postmodern', goes one step further and implies that documentary itself is a mode with no special claim to 'truth' or 'reality', but is rather 'merely "an image" and *not* an authentic representation' (1997: 45). On the face of it, the 'relativist' dimension of postmodernism seems ideally suited to animation as a form: it could be argued that any animated documentary, freed as it is from the indexicality of the live-action/photographed image, allows the animator's 'subjectivity' to automatically question some of the certainties of the 'objective' discourse of documentary as a form. However, while it is important to recognise the inherently constructed nature of animated documentaries, this does not mean that we can make the leap to state that any and all truth claims or observations made by animated documentaries can be dismissed as 'relative' or 'merely' a product of the animator's point of view or subjectivity. The formal and aesthetic aspects of animation tend to mean that the creativity and subjectivity of the creator are considerably more foregrounded than is often the case with live-action work; nevertheless, the claims made about the real world of actuality by animated documentaries must be evaluated according to what they say about that real world, and not on the basis of such formal or aesthetic criteria.

As was made clear in chapter one, constructing typologies, or thinking about how and where specific examples might fit on a continuum, are very useful things to do, as they emphasise the *relative* relationships between modes. Therefore, one must recognise that there are no definite answers here. Indeed, it can be suggested (and Wells would surely not disagree) that there is considerable overlap between the four modes outlined above and, certainly, there are some animated documentaries that arguably use more than one mode. With documentary, we are dealing with what Carl Plantinga refers to as an 'open concept' (see chapter one). It is no coincidence that one of the most interesting books in the area of documentary studies is entitled *Blurred Boundaries*, and that it openly engages with the ways that fiction and nonfiction inter-relate and overlap. (Though interestingly, Bill Nichols makes no mention of animation as a form.) The notion of 'prototypicality' (something that Plantinga borrows from George Lakoff) is of central importance here (and to arguments advanced in other chapters in this book – see chapters one and two in particular). What this suggests is that we might well strive to define and pin down what something 'is', but actual examples will tend not to 'tick all the boxes' of a particular definition. So it is with both animation and documentary: there are some examples that appear to fall right in the middle of these categories; they fulfil all the ostensible criteria. There are other examples that appear to be on the periphery, to 'not quite fit'. In many respects, my main argument throughout this book is that thinking about such examples and how they relate to others is one of the best ways of understanding the entire field. It is certainly the case that, as Gunnar Strom states, 'the term "animated documentary" may seem like a contradiction' (2003: 47), but the more we examine the interface between these two apparently opposed poles, the more useful their interaction becomes for understanding how both modes operate.

Representing the real in an unreal way: the contradictory nature of animated documentary

Although there are clearly a range of styles and techniques used in both animation and documentary, it has to be said that there is something inherently 'reflexive' about animation, especially in relation to documentary. In Wells' typology of modes, even the imitative mode holds a strange position in the sense that even the most 'realistic' of animation (for example, something from the 'hyper-realist' style of Disney) will be watched *as* animation, rather than as a 'recording' of an actual pro-filmic world. That is, despite any truth claims made, or real-world situations and relationships shown, the 'animatedness' will still be an overriding feature of the film for the viewer as they watch the film. This is not to say that the claims made or situations represented are thereby somehow completely invalidated – on the contrary, it might well be the case that an animated documentary manages to reveal *more* of the 'reality' of a situation than any number of live-action documentaries. But the ontological status of the images (the sounds are arguably of a different order, and this issue is returned to below) means that the perceptions of 'animatedness' and 'documentariness' are in conflict to a large degree. This is not necessarily a problem: such conflict is arguably a requirement for any form of expression that wants to engage with the real world in all its complexity and contradiction.

In an essay about documentary and animation, Sybil Del Gaudio examines what she calls the 'reflexive' mode (one that differs slightly from that proposed by Nichols in relation to live-action documentary), focusing in particular on some documentaries that 'use animation to deal with scientific theory'; she argues that 'such films serve as a means by which a filmmaker can question the adequacy of representation in relationship to that which it represents' (1997: 197). In other words, the very constructedness of the animation forces the 'reflection' on form and meaning that is central to a 'reflexive' mode, something that sometimes gets lost in the seductively mimetic world of live action. This is another role that animation fulfils (along with the straightforward 'simplification' of complex processes that we might see in training and educational films that use animation – see Crafton 1993: 158): drawing attention to the specific signifying practices of certain documentaries.

One common feature of a significant number of animated documentaries is their tendency to use animation techniques to explicitly represent and interpret the thoughts and feelings of their subjects. There are two main reasons for this 'subjective' tendency. First of all, in this context we are often talking about highly abstract feelings, or taboos, or are dealing with people who find it difficult to articulate. Secondly, there are some issues relating to anonymity – animation offers a 'cloak' that live action might not: as we are dealing with direct testimony we are effectively seeing these people's thoughts and feelings visualised. There are of course other conventions for representing someone who might wish to remain anonymous – the chief example being the 'silhouette' style testimony – but such approaches do not offer the creative freedom that animation affords.

For example, in the short series of animated documentaries, *Animated Minds* (directed by Andy Glynne, 2003, UK) we hear the spoken testimony of real sufferers from various mental illnesses, accompanied by animated visuals. The individual films are *Fish on a Hook* (panic attacks and agoraphobia), *Dimensions* (schizophrenia), *Obsessively Compulsive* (obsessive compulsive disorder), and *That Light Bulb Thing* (manic depression); each film has a very different style. In *Dimensions*, for example, we hear the voice of a man who tells us of his experiences of suffering from psychotic interludes. The animation techniques used here tend towards a fragmentary, 'overlaid' look, where elements of a recognisably external reality (newspaper headlines, London Underground tunnels) are fused and altered to reflect the mentality of the speaker. At the onset of the disorder, the voiceover tells us:

> Initially the experiences were quite positive; I was living outside consensus reality ... [with a] very heightened sense of awareness ... delusions of grandeur, which are quite pleasant.

It then cuts to a newspaper, and he says 'so, I'd open up a newspaper and I'd think it would all refer to me'. The headline 'Okri for Booker Prize' then dissolves/morphs to read 'Young genius writes debut novel'. Similarly, people on the radio were imagined to be speaking to him directly. During both of these sequences, the animated backgrounds are fragmentary and shifting (trees, power pylons, the aforementioned headlines), but the colours and motion do not really imply threat. As the speaker says, it was all 'quite pleasant'.

As the affliction became more oppressive, we hear that he started to hear voices – often recognisably those of his sister, father, mother – encouraging him to self-harm. As things get more and more disturbing, the animation consists of eerily shifting human silhouettes and subliminal messages that flash up too quickly for the eye to register, saying 'WHY

DON'T YOU SLIT YOURSELF? ... 'YEAH ... IT'S EASY ... GO ON.' The shift to an alternate reality is almost complete: 'I do find it amazing, the power of the human brain, that it can recreate ... ten, twenty voices perfectly', so much so that he 'could never imagine the old, normal reality coming back'.

Obviously, one could make a live-action documentary about this affliction and include testimony of the person involved. But it is the use of animation that is interesting, as it can perfectly trace the contours of such a shifting and rapidly condensed thought process in a way that is out of reach for live action. Animation is the perfect way in which to communicate that there is more to our collective experience of things than meets the eye. As suggested elsewhere regarding rotoscoped films, the recent work of Bob Sabiston in particular (Ward 2004; 2005b; forthcoming), it can be argued that animated films offer us an *intensified* route into understanding the real social world, by virtue of the peculiar dialectic that is set up between knowing that this is a film about a real person (and we can hear their *actual* voice) and knowing that what we are looking at is an animated construction, with nothing of the indexical correspondence that we have become so accustomed to. The animation techniques used are a clear example of the 'creative treatment of actuality' – such that John Grierson would no doubt find animated documentaries something of a logical conclusion to his famous definition.

In *Obsessively Compulsive*, the interviewee talks about his struggles to come to terms with obsessive compulsive disorder (OCD). The main symptom in this person's case is an inability to carry out even the simplest of day-to-day tasks (walking across a room, drinking a cup of tea) without an 'intrusive thought' breaking in and preventing the completion of the task. In this particular person's case, his intrusive thoughts were concerned with Saddam Hussain: whenever he thought about Saddam, he worried that his thinking about him was causing the Gulf War to escalate. This then led to him obsessing over his inability *not* to think about Saddam. The animation techniques used draw a clear connection between the 'real world' people and events and the ways in which they can quickly become part of a deluded fantasy world. It is this 'subjectivising' of elements of actuality that some might find problematic – but it is equally clear that the film is documenting the mental processes inherent in such a disorder. The use of stop-motion, 'looped' animation of an actor, while we hear the real voice of the OCD-sufferer, emphasises the repetitive, cyclical nature of

Figure 7 *Obsessively Compulsive* (2003)

OCD. The final image of the film perfectly captures this motif: the camera tracks back to reveal a cross-section of a 'compartmentalised' head, with each compartment containing an animated version of the man obsessively performing an action.

A different technique is used in the mainly live-action film *Feeling Space* (Iain Piercy, 1999, UK), but the objective is similar: to try and visualise what a sensation (or lack of it) is like. This film uses animated sequences at certain points to represent the thoughts and feelings of two men, Brian Baistow and Tommy Cannon, who were born blind, describing their journeys through Glasgow. At one point they talk about how 'road signs' for blind people might helpfully consist of a street-side sculpture at ground level that they can feel the texture of in order to ascertain where they are, what buildings are around them, and so on. As they speak of the cityscape, however, shots of buildings are 'cloaked' by animated blank sheets, until they are featureless blocks. This works as a strong visual metaphor for something most of us take for granted – the ability to see, the wonder of architecture that surrounds us – but what makes this work as a documentary is the linking to the *specific* experiences of the two speakers. The two men describe in some detail the textures, sounds and smells of Glasgow, and how they feel at various points. The animation functions as a way to visualise (ironically enough) something that would otherwise remain at the purely verbal level. But it is in the rendering of the realities of these two people's day-to-day lives that the film develops as a documentary. In common with the other films discussed in this chapter, we are given insight into something we would otherwise not know anything about, let alone understand. The animation used exists as a contrast, something that draws out and emphasises the shortcomings of conventional live-action representations of what the world is like. The long-standing assumption about documentaries is that they reveal to us what something 'is like' by showing, or by observing. The indexical link between the pro-filmic actuality and the imagery that appears in the documentary is a very strong one; however, in the case of *Feeling Space*, we (the viewers) are seeing what the subjects of the film cannot see, and they are experiencing their milieu in a way that we cannot, by virtue of actually being able to see it. It is this paradox that is creatively addressed by the animated sequences in the film: an attempt to document the undocumentable.

The animation tendencies seen in all of these examples come under what Paul Wells has termed 'penetrative animation', following John Halas and Joy Batchelor's use of the term. Here, penetration refers to animation's

ability to evoke the internal space and portray the invisible. Abstract concepts and previously unimaginable states can be visualised through animation in ways that are difficult to achieve or which remain unpersuasive in the live-action context. (1998: 122)

Thus, the states of mind documented in the *Animated Minds* films, *Feeling Space*, or Tim Webb's landmark film *A is for Autism* become *easier* to understand as a consequence of their animatedness. Webb's film uses the drawings of actual autistic people, animating them while the various people reflect on their autism on the soundtrack. The fact that autism is not one 'thing' but rather is a spectrum of disorders (from mild to severe) makes the subjectivised, 'individual' strands of different animation techniques (as well as live-action montage) a highly appropriate mode for representing it. The film works as a documentary precisely because of its 'hybrid' aesthetic. In attempting to represent to the viewer a hidden or masked reality – what is it like, subjectively, for your subjectivity to play 'tricks' on you? – *A is for Autism* draws out some of the problems and contradictions of trying to represent the 'real world' in the first place. One of the characteristics of autism is a tendency to take things that are said very literally, and for 'commonsense' ways of looking at the world to be far from sensible. People with autism are often thought to be intellectually deficient or unable to communicate 'properly', but more often than not, their apparent deficiency is merely them looking at the world in a way that is very different from 'the norm'. In the film, one person reflects on the soundtrack that if someone points something out to them that they find interesting, they might not be able to 'see' it, even if it is obviously 'there', and that they might seem to be 'distracted' by irrelevant things. As they put it: 'I always have trouble "finding" it ... [but] I can see something boring straight away.' Such a statement raises all sorts of issues for visual representation, yet Webb manages to brilliantly convey this problem by using one of the speaker's own drawings, inverting it, and animating it. Within the drawing, a car repetitively moves backwards and forwards next to a tree, but does so at the top of the frame, upside down, rather than at the bottom of the frame. In another part of the drawing, some figures walk round what looks like a rocket (though it may be a church). There are also some random squiggly lines, moving about in yet another part of the picture. As we hear the speaker, the image inverts so that the car is the 'right way up', and the camera zooms in on it. Doing this means that things that were previously the right way up are now 'wrong', however. As the speaker talks of being able to 'see something boring straight away', the camera zooms into the mess of the squiggly lines. This underlines the visual 'confusion' that the speaker refers to, and is an effective way of communicating this to the viewer.

It is no coincidence that *A is for Autism* uses as a basis the drawings of actual sufferers from autism. This, then, is another common feature of animated documentaries that is worth stressing: the tendency towards collaborative working methods or, at the very least, methods that draw in the subjects in a way that is rarely seen or felt to the same extent in the live-action documentary context. *A is for Autism* is called 'a collaboration' in its opening credits. Bob Sabiston's short film *Snack and Drink* (1999, US), which uses his computer rotoscoping technique 'Rotoshop' to visualise the mindset of Ryan Power, an autistic teenager featured in the film, includes some sequences that were animated by Power's mother and aunt.[3] It is this hands-on involvement of the subjects of these films in the actual production process that makes animated documentaries poten-

Figure 8 *Snack & Drink* (1999)

tially very interesting. Indeed, an early version of Bill Nichols' typology of documentary modes (discussed in chapter one) includes the 'interactive' documentary and a significant number of animated documentaries can be said to be 'interactive' in this sense. As noted in chapter one, Nichols describes the interactive documentary as a category where 'images of testimony or verbal exchange' feature heavily, and there is an emphasis on 'various forms of monologue and dialogue' (1991: 44). In other words, unlike, say, the expository mode (with its use of 'voice of God' exposition) or the observational mode (with its use of 'fly-on-the-wall' techniques) the interactive documentary tends to rely on the filmmaker's interaction with their subjects, most often embodied in the form of an interview. Thus, the testimony or forms of monologue/dialogue become the main focus for 'interactive' documentaries (see Ward, forthcoming). Furthermore, as noted above, many of the animated documentaries discussed here are also interactive in the sense that the subjects themselves will often inter-act with the animator by becoming involved in the production process. This is, of course, a vital point to make when we consider that the topics of these films are precisely the supposedly incommunicable thoughts and concepts about what it is like to be blind, autistic and so on. These films could not really exist without the express involvement of the people they 'are about'. Clearly this can be said of any documentary, but it is never truer than with these films, and it is in their 'interactive' and 'penetrative' representing of a worldview that they push back the boundaries of documentary signification.

A related term to the 'penetrative' as outlined above is the 'optical unconscious'. This term is borrowed from Walter Benjamin (1979) and it is very useful for understanding how we might 'see' and understand things that are not immediately apprehendable simply by looking. There is a difference in the sense that the 'optical unconscious' was Benjamin's way of theorising how certain techniques – for example, magnification, inversion – might 'make strange' the familiar things that surround us and make people see the world in a new and different way. This is different to 'penetration' in the sense that the latter is focusing on how certain techniques – animation, in particular – might penetrate beneath the surface of something (for example, a social process such as banking) and reveal 'how it works'. But the two concepts are closely related. The 'optical unconscious' is a useful term for understanding how certain animation renders the dream state to spectators (Ward 2005b), yet what is of interests here is how animation techniques (and it should of course be remembered that there are many kinds of animation technique) in some sense get beneath the apparent certainties of mere appearance. Such a move should again remind us of Grierson's exhortation to 'creatively treat' actuality rather than merely 'reproduce' it.

Of course, the notion of attempting to foreground an 'optical unconscious' can be seen as merely one strategy amongst many others that might be termed 'modernist' in the political, revelatory sense of that term. The point of such an 'unconscious' is to delineate and understand how the world 'really works', rather than merely accepting it and taking it at face value. Bearing this in mind, we can see how the use of animation techniques to represent aspects of the real world offers a route into dissecting the taken-for-granted assumptions that underpin our understanding of that world. For example, Emily James uses a collage of found footage, animation, puppets and other stop-motion techniques in order to construct a critique of unfair globalised trading in *The Luckiest Nut in the World* (2002, UK). As

Mike Wayne points out, this film 'illuminate[s] the yawning contradiction between what the discourse of neo-liberalism imposes on Third World countries as a route out of poverty and the actual outcomes, which turn out to be more poverty' (2003: 230–1). Likewise, Karen Watson's animated film about child abuse, *Daddy's Little Bit of Dresden China* (1988, UK) uses a range of animation techniques, along with a combination of 'real' and 'acted' voices in order to explore the hypocrisy and contradictions inherent in certain 'commonsense' assumptions about this social taboo. The apparent sanctity of the family unit – along with the 'Othering' of abusers (the myth that they are always strangers rather than family members) – means that in commonsense discourse, it becomes impossible to talk about the issue in any meaningful way. In the same way that the World Bank and the International Monetary Fund are the engineers of the very problems they say they are trying to solve, so it is with the problems in *Daddy's Little Bit of Dresden China*, where the apparent safety of family life is revealed to be a sham. It is impossible to offer a critique of these two social problems without recognising the contradiction that lies at their heart, and the use of animation does much to address this contradiction. As Wayne states in relation to *The Luckiest Nut in the World*:

> The immanent critique of a concept like 'trade liberalisation' is also then a critique and reworking of the generic materials of mass culture whose 'innocence' and naivety are juxtaposed (with comic and tragic effect) with brutal realities. (2003: 231)

In other words, it is in the very form that the material takes that we can discern critique. *Daddy's Little Bit of Dresden China* for example, makes great (ironic) play of invoking fairytales, as well as other 'mass' or 'folk' forms (for example, the tabloid press and the 'commonsense' beliefs it tends to peddle) in order to draw out the ways in which these forms are often complicit in the continuation of a social problem. The bravura sequence in the pub, where voices on the soundtrack jostle with one another to condemn paedophiles while the animation literally tears away layers, and the men 'eye up' the barmaid, shows brilliantly the hypocrisy that underpins much commonsense or populist discourse on the matter.

The complexity of the sound-image relations in *Daddy's Little Bit of Dresden China* is in fact a common feature of many animated documentaries. There is 'realism' or indexicality to the sound that does not reside in the image, and it is this more than anything else that helps to make animated documentaries of considerable critical importance. A large number of films in the animated documentary category consist of voice tracks that are recordings of real conversations, interviews, or pseudo-monologues which are then 'creatively interpreted' by the animated imagery. For example, the 'confessional' we hear in Aardman's *Going Equipped* (Peter Lord, 1989, UK) consists of a young man talking about his experiences as a burglar. While we hear the real man talking on the soundtrack, we see a combination of stylised live-action footage (showing things like the squalor of his home life) and a claymation figure in a room who 'speaks' the words we hear. This is an example of what Michael Renov (2004) has referred to as 'acoustic indexicality' in relation to the soundtracks of animated documentaries. His discussion of Australian animator Dennis Tupicoff's film *His Mother's Voice* (1997, Aus.) stresses the ways in which the animated visuals 'creatively interpret' an 'authentic' soundtrack. Kathy Easdale's son Matthew was shot dead in Brisbane in 1995 and the film's soundtrack consists of a recording of the Australian Broadcasting Corporation's radio interview with her, talking about how she felt when she heard about her son's death. Tupicoff draws attention to the fact that a real soundtrack can be interpreted in very different ways by playing the interview twice but changing the visuals – the first time we see a rotoscoped re-enactment of some of the events from the evening of the shooting, the second time we hear the interview we start in a room with Kathy Easdale and the interviewer, but the camera soon departs to roam around outside the house while she continues to emotionally remember the events. As Emru Townsend points out:

> Tupicoff ... says, 'By presenting just two of the many possible points of view that might accompany the voice of Mrs Kathy Easdale, I hope the film leaves the audience to imagine others, and to ponder its own response to her pain.' The film itself tells the audience that what we see is not an absolute; the same events, narrated by the same person, can be observed, interpreted and experienced in many different ways. (1998: n.p.)

This goes right to the heart of why animated documentaries are vitally important: because they often use this trope of a 'real' soundtrack – interview, snatches of dialogue and so on – that is then creatively interpreted by the animated visuals. As the viewer can be under *no* illusion that what they are looking at is, categorically, a construction, then this prompts them to consider the *nature* of that construction, and its relation to the sounds we are hearing. This is something that is often taken for granted in relation to live-action documentaries, with the apparent 'naturalness' of the link between image and sound. The question that is implicitly asked here is: if someone is speaking about something, should we be watching *them*; or perhaps we should be watching a *re-enacted version* of what they are talk-ing about; or watching an *animated version* of what they are talking about; or, perhaps we should simply leave the room and wander around outside, taking in the view? The assumption that documentary visuals should merely 'illustrate' the sound (or conversely, that documentary sound should act as nothing more than a 'back up' to the images) is critically foregrounded by animated documentaries in general. Indeed, as this chapter has suggested, animated documentaries should receive more scholarly attention, as they potentially provide answers to some of the more troubling questions asked of documentary as a field.

CONCLUSION: THE FUTURE OF DOCUMENTARY

It is clear that documentary as a category is now as vibrant and dynamic as it has ever been – both on the small and large screens. This is partly due to the ways in which those practitioners working in the field have responded to the changing climate of deregulation (particularly in the UK), and means that there are some fascinating recent trends in documentary and factual filmmaking. Much has been made of the ways that reality TV has effectively lessened the impact and importance of documentary, because it has used the serious and sober aims associated with documentary in the service of a watered-down, ratings-seeking philosophy, more driven by entertainment. Likewise, there have been some worries voiced that new technologies (the almost complete manipulation of the image afforded by digital technology, for example) are changing the way documentaries are made and viewed – and not necessarily for the better.

However, I would argue that the vibrancy of the area means that examples are consistently appearing that actually make us rethink precisely what 'documentary' might mean, rather than simply debasing or diluting it. For example, a current tendency is for documentaries to make extensive use of computer-generated imagery (CGI) and other forms of digital 'trickery'. *Walking With Dinosaurs* (BBC, 2000, UK) used digital technology to show in hyper-realistic detail what life might have been like during pre-historic times. There have also been documentaries where CGI is used instead of dramatic reconstruction – to show the last moments of Pompeii, as Vesuvius erupted, for instance. As the discussion of animated documentaries in chapter five suggested, one of the key shifts in recent times has been the increased tendency for documentaries to consist of images that do not have an indexical link to the thing they purport to show. This arguably represents a major theoretical and philosophical challenge to commonsense definitions of documentary as a mode: is it possible for us to refer to something as a 'documentary' if it is completely computer-rendered, for instance? Or does a documentary necessarily require indexical images from the real world? A related issue here is the 'speculative' nature of such films and programmes – what we could call the 'might have been' factor. The CGI of *Walking With Dinosaurs* and the like is only ever going to be a 'best guess', and is this as good as an actual *record* of something? As argued throughout this book, a dramatised reconstruction (or, indeed, a CGI rendering) of something is obviously of a different order than imagery that is clearly captured at the time the events happened, but this does not necessarily mean that the former cannot have some 'documentary value', to paraphrase Grierson. It all depends on how this imagery is deployed in the film or programme, and how the audience interprets it. It is more in these viewing contexts that the meaning of documentary resides, than in any essential features of the documentaries themselves.

One of the other more encouraging recent developments has been the ability of people to make documentaries very cheaply and, perhaps more crucially, find ways of getting them to a reasonably large audience. As television has abdicated some of its responsibilities in this area (either by simply not commissioning more challenging work in the fear it will not win the ratings war, or by relegating such work to minority channels, like BBC4 in the UK), there have been a number of notable successes in cinemas and alternative channels of distribution. Campaigning, issue-driven films such as *The Corporation* (Jennifer Abbott and Mark Achbar, 2003, US) and *Super Size Me* (Morgan Spurlock, 2004, US)have achieved success in cinemas. The former film's sell-through on DVD is being handled using grass-roots/ activist techniques, perfectly in keeping with the underlying message of the film. Documentaries made by Robert Greenwald – such as *Outfoxed: Rupert Murdoch's War on Journalism* (2004, US), about the partisan nature of Fox News Network in the US – have circumvented any problems with distribution by distributing the film on DVD, direct to viewers. These examples, as well as the still-emerging role of the internet in the dissemination of news/actuality and documentary material, mean that we will have to deal with the notion of documentary for some time to come.

Central to this book has been the notion that documentary has close relationships with other forms of expression – drama/fiction, comedy, animation – and that we need to think carefully about how these relationships might have changed what we think documentary can be. The most interesting work being done in the field at the moment is that which engages with these relationships, and thinks through how documentary 'interfaces' with other modes of expression. A recent film such as *Tarnation* (Jonathan Caouette, 2003, US) for example, makes a virtue of its fractured-ness and hybridity, constructing a compelling documentary from the highly personal fragments of a life – photographs, answering-machine messages and so on. However, it is clear that the notion of *performance* is still central to this film: it is a deeply personal 'performing' of a life, as self-indulgent as it is compelling. Equally clear is that such a film (apparently made for $218 and edited on home computer) shows that virtually anyone can make a documentary that might have a large impact. In this respect, *Tarnation* and films like it are the flipside of the hugely expensive 'digi-docs', where CGI is used to render and document worlds that would otherwise remain invisible, or be brought to the screen using more traditional means such as talking heads or dramatic reconstruction. With *Tarnation*, digital technology is being used to 'democratise' the process, and make things more affordable. The consequence of this might be that there will be an upsurge in deeply personal films such as this, where the ephemera of people's lives (favourite songs, jottings from a notebook) become the basis for a new kind of documentary. One thing is certain: because documentaries tell stories about the real world, they will always be part of that world, and will need to keep evolving with it.

NOTES

Introduction

1 It is not often noted that although Grierson uses the term 'documentary', here the context of the quote is as follows: 'Of course, *Moana* being a visual account of events in the daily life of a Polynesian youth and his family, has documentary value. But that, I believe, is secondary to its value as a soft breath from a sunlit island washed by a marvelous sea as warm as the balmy air. *Moana* is first of all beautiful as nature is beautiful...' The 'documentary value' that the film has is seen as a *subsidiary* element, with the main worth of the film residing, for Grierson, in its 'poetry'.

Chapter one

1 It should be added here that filming in one long take, and/or not using any sound are of course editing and sound 'choices' in the sense that any viewer would find them eminently noticeable and think about why the filmmaker had chosen to use such (non-)conventions.

2 The phrase originally appeared in his 1933 article 'The Documentary Producer', *Cinema Quarterly*, 2, 1, 8.

3 In this respect, one could argue that *Chronique d'un ete* is a reflexive documentary, and this is precisely what Jay Ruby does in his essay 'The Image Mirrored: Reflexivity and the Documentary Film' (in Rosenthal 1988).

4 Quoted in Emma Perry (2001) 'In the frame: Little ups and downs', *Time Out*, 20–27 June.

5 Of course, this 'change of direction' would surely have been planned from the outset – which is to say, Isaacs probably had a hunch that most people might respond in the ways they did, starting out shy of the camera, then gradually

'opening up' for it.

6   We can, of course, have nonfictional musicals.

7   As Plantinga points out, it is entirely possible to watch a fiction film nonfiction-ally – that is, to infer some 'real world' knowledge from viewing it. This is what happens if someone were to watch *The Matrix* with a view to charting Keanu Reeves' acting career, or the use of certain special effects. In this respect, the (fiction) film is viewed as a real-world artefact, it is comprehended nonfiction-ally. But there is a difference between this specific kind of *usage* and actual properties of the nonfictional, as Plantinga makes clear. One might view a fiction film in this way for particular purposes, but the general (or conven-tional) use and understanding of the film is an entirely different thing. One-off (mis)understandings are different from socially agreed usage, and it is this latter category which is vital when we are defining something like 'documen-tary' or 'nonfiction'.

8   Of course, there is a 'preferred' way of doing things in the sense of there being a recognised professional way of conducting an interview. This raises all sorts of issues about the relationship of discourses of 'professionalism' to modes of documentary (and other filmmaking) practices. It should also be noted at this point that some documentarists would not *necessarily* agree that inter-views are an integral part of documentary. For example, someone like Godfrey Reggio makes films that completely dispense with interviews or voiceover.

Chapter two

1   By pointing to such 'uncertainty' on the part of the viewer, it is not suggested that viewers are duped or fooled into simply thinking they are watching a doc-umentary or a drama when this is manifestly not the case. A lot of the time viewers are well aware that what they are watching is a documentary that is attempting to mobilise drama or performance in some 'new' way, and they will watch the material while negotiating precisely this point. There might be some initial 'literal' uncertainty, but most people watch things having some prior knowledge of the conventions and mode of address involved, and will respond accordingly. Much more research is needed into viewer responses to types of documentary output. See Austin 2005b.

2   Two of the actors were recognisable to me personally. This is not necessar-ily a problem, though it is interesting to think through some of the differ-ent 'responses' that spectators might have to such material, depending on whether they 'spot' that it is an actor playing the role. For, even if one *knows* that a film like *Pissed on the Job* is addressing viewers in the way that it does – that is, as a 'documentary-style', performed interpretation of detailed inter-

view material – it is pretty likely that one still attaches more 'authenticity' to an 'unknown' face than someone one knows to be so-and-so, the actor. This is actually a strange paradox of sorts, where we can recognise the skill and 'authenticity' of someone's performance, but if we 'know' them from a previous film or programme, then it disrupts this admiration. This only really happens when actors are performing in the documentary arena – or the new, hybridised, performed documentaries. *Pissed on the Job* used professional actors (albeit less well-known ones), Woolcock's *Tina* films used non-professional actors (or 'real people') improvising variations on themselves. A similar paradox is at work with mock-doc texts such as *The Office*, where we know that the characters are being acted – there is admiration (and cringing recognition) of the authenticity, yet this has to co-exist with admiration of the quality of the performances. The more praise the series received for its authenticity, the more recognition there was of the virtuosity of the acted performances.

3   'Perceived as' being the key phrase – although modern viewers might perceive *A Job in a Million* to be stilted, we should not assume that the audience of 1937 felt the same way.

Chapter three

1   For a detailed account of the production process for the re-enactment, see the relevant Historical Film Services pages: http://www.historicalfilmservices.com/orgreave.htm.

2   The Nottinghamshire collieries saw a large number of miners returning to work while the strike was still on. Some Nottinghamshire miners maintain that because there had been no national ballot on strike action, they were legitimately going back to work. However, this fails to see their actions as part of a wider context of working-class solidarity – as the Yorkshire miners in *The Battle of Orgreave* clearly feel, the fact that some of the Nottinghamshire miners were back at work while the strike was still on sent a message to the Thatcher government, who were obviously on a well-planned collision-course with the National Union of Mineworkers.

3   Julian Petley has pointed out to me that he remembers that the ITN news on the same evening actually showed these events in the correct order. This is one of the reasons that the furore over the BBC's doctoring of the sequence rose to such a pitch. If the miners had been the only ones pointing out that there was a clear distortion occurring, they would doubtless have simply been ignored. But it was difficult for the authorities to completely ignore the issue when Britain's most respected news producers (the BBC and ITN) showed completely contradictory sequences of the same events.

4   Interviewed on *Newsnight* on 27 July 1984, Margaret Thatcher talked of the miners and picket line violence as follows: '[If] any government gave in to the violence and intimidation of the kind which has disfigured our screens, there would be no future for democracy ... the violence and intimidation we have seen should never have happened. It is the work of extremists. It is the enemy within.' Figgis ironically juxtaposes Thatcher's words on the soundtrack with the ominous build-up of militarily-ranked police officers, with the result that the police (and by extension Thatcher herself) become the 'extremists', 'the enemy within'. Later in the film, the 'enemy within' soundbite is repeated over tracking shots of now-derelict mining communities and boarded-up shops – more in sadness than irony.

5   The 'Acid Brass' project (1997) was a series of concerts and a recording by the Williams Fairey Band playing Brass Band interpretations of acid house music. Deller juxtaposed these two forms of music without irony, as he saw them both as popular, 'folk' forms of music. The links between the two forms – and how they can and should be seen in a broad context of recent working-class history and culture – are explored further in Deller's *The History of the World 1997–2004* (2004, UK). This is a large flow diagram showing the mass of inter-connections between the two.

6   See http://www.folkarchive.co.uk

7   The inquest was initially called to investigate the death of John Lees, and the powers that be had every reason to believe that it would be an open and shut case. In this respect, those who spoke up against the actions of the Yeomanry were going against the grain of what was expected – that is, they were not called specifically as witnesses 'against' the Yeomanry, and would more than likely be expected not to speak out – and they took the inquest in an unexpected direction as a consequence.

Chapter four

1   Of course, *The Office* also comes to its audience 'indexed' (see chapter one) as a mock-docu-soap, and the presence of a recognisable performer such as Ricky Gervais anchors this further.

2   See, for example, some of the customer reviews for the DVD of the film on Amazon.com (http://www.amazon.com/exec/obidos/gdetail//0767846869/104-6698739-3642360?v=glance); or viewer comments at the Internet Movie Database (http://www.imdb.com/title/tt0181288/usercomments?start=0).

3   See, for example, *Man Bites Dog* (Remy Belvaux, André Bonzel, Benoît Poelvoorde, 1992, Bel.). This film is a mock-documentary, and is, in places, very funny. But it is a very dark, mordant satire on media journalists' standards

and ethics, which uses an accurate parody of a documentary team following a serial killer as the vehicle for its broader critical points.

4   The programme invented a drug ('Cake is a made-up drug...') and some moral panic-style stories about its effects and then asked various celebrities to condemn the drug.

Chapter five

1   The series, *Blood Matters*, was a four-part series examining aspects of blood and blood donation, made by various directors and animators under the aegis of the Documentary Filmmakers Group, in association with the National Blood Service. The other films were more 'personal' or specifically focused on an issue such as the relatively low donation rate amongst ethnic minorities. As such, they tended to use less straightforwardly 'expository' techniques and be more 'subjective' or 'poetic' in the way they engaged with blood donation as a real world issue. The films are: *What's Blood Got To Do With It?* (directed by Andy Glynne; animation director – Jim Field); *Leona. Alone* (directed by Rani Khanna; animation director – Benji Davies); *Blood Sutra* (directed by Rajesh Thind; animation director – Ravi Swami); *The Circle* (directed by Caroline Gardiner; animation directors – Gemma Carrington and Alon Ziv).

2   This is not to say that there is no such thing as the 'objective' world 'out there', independent of us and about which we can have (at least partial) knowledge. But it is to claim that there are considerable problems with an 'objective' discourse in the sense that it is often (incorrectly) mobilised in relation to documentary: that is, as a standpoint that is 'fair', 'balanced' and so on. Such 'objectivity' is what Stuart Hall would refer to as 'an operational fiction' (1988: 361), and it is precisely such simplistic thoughts of objectivity that are shaken by the subjectivity of animated documentaries.

3   See Sabiston's notes on the film at: http://www.abm-medien.de/filmbuero/ snack_e.htm. For more on *Snack and Drink* and the combination of animation and documentary see Ward, forthcoming.

BIBLIOGRAPHY

Essential reading

Bruzzi, Stella (2000) *New Documentary: A Critical Introduction*. London: Routledge. *Incisive critique of documentary traditions, examining mainly post-1960s material.*

Grierson, John (1966) *Grierson on Documentary*. Edited and compiled by Forsyth Hardy. Berkeley: University of California Press. *Collection of articles by Grierson, exploring specific techniques and conventions, but also discussing the role of documentary, possibilities for distribution, and so forth.*

Lipkin, Steven N. (2002) *Real Emotional Logic: Film and Television Docudrama as Persuasive Practice*. Carbondale and Edwardsville: Southern Illinois University Press. *Very useful attempt to discuss docudrama as a form of argument; interesting outline of relationship between fiction and nonfiction.*

Nichols, Bill (1991) *Representing Reality*. Bloomington and Indianapolis: Indiana University Press. *Excellent overview of theoretical concepts relating to documentary modes.*

_____ (2001) *Introduction to Documentary*. Bloomington and Indianapolis: Indiana University Press. *Key terms and concepts summarised in an accessible format where each chapter heading consists of a straightforward question (for example, 'What are documentaries about?', 'What types of documentary are there?')*

Paget, Derek (1998) *No Other Way To Tell It: Dramadoc/docudrama on Television*. Manchester: Manchester University Press. *Outlines the key terms and concepts for understanding the relationship and overlap between drama and documentary as modes.*

Plantinga, Carl (1997) *Rhetoric and Representation in Nonfiction Film*. Cambridge: Cambridge University Press.

An intelligent account of the signifying practices of nonfiction films, examining how they represent the real world, make assertions, and persuade their audiences.

Roscoe, Jane and Craig Hight (2001) *Faking It: Mock-documentary and the Subversion of Factuality*. Manchester: Manchester University Press.

Useful account of the mock-documentary, attempting to construct a typology of the form as well as examine how such texts relate to 'proper' documentary.

Rosenthal, Alan (ed.) (1988) *New Challenges for Documentary*. Berkeley: University of California Press.

One of the best anthologies on documentary, covering a very wide range of material by some of the best writers and practitioners in the field.

Winston, Brian (1995) *Claiming the Real: The Documentary Film Revisited*. London: British Film Institute.

Excellent critical engagement with the central tenets of Grierson's phrase, 'the creative treatment of actuality', ranging across a variety of documentary modes.

Secondary reading

Altman, Rick (1999) *Film/Genre*. London: British Film Institute.

Austin, Thomas (2005a) 'Seeing, Feeling, Knowing: A Case Study of Audience Perspectives on Screen Documentary', *Particip@tions* 2, 1. Available online: http://www.particapations.org/volume%202/issue%201/2_01_austin.htm.

_____ (2005b) 'Family, class, perversion: *Capturing the Friedmans*', unpublished article.

Barnouw, Eric (1993) *Documentary: A History of the Non-Fiction Film* (second edition). Oxford: Oxford University Press.

Barsam, Richard Meran (1992) *Nonfiction Film: A Critical History* (second edition). Indiana and Bloomington: Indiana University Press.

Benjamin, Walter (1973) *Illuminations*. London: Fontana.

_____ (1979) 'A Small History of Photography', in *One-Way Street and Other Writings*. London: New Left Books, 240–57.

Bennett, Catherine (2000) 'Beware of cheap imitation', *Guardian*, 3 February. Available online: http://www.guardian.co.uk/shipman/Story/0,2763,192666,00.html.

Biressi, Anita and Heather Nunn (2005) *Reality TV: Realism and Revelation*. London: Wallflower Press.

Bowker, Geoffrey C. and Susan Leigh Star (1999) *Sorting Things Out: Classification and its Consequences*. Cambridge, MA: MIT Press.

Carroll, Noël (1996) 'Nonfiction Film and Postmodernist Skepticism', in David Bordwell and Noël Carroll (eds) *Post-Theory: Reconstructing Film Studies*. Madison: University of Wisconsin Press, 283–306.

Cawelti, John G. (1985) 'Chinatown and Generic Transformation in Recent American Films', in Gerald Mast and Marshall Cohen (eds) *Film Theory and Criticism*. Oxford: Oxford University Press, 559–79.

Corner, John (1996) *The Art of Record*. Manchester: Manchester University Press.

____ (2000) 'Documentary in a Post-Documentary Culture? A Note on Forms and their Functions', Working Paper No. 1 in the 'Changing Media–Changing Europe' series, published by Loughborough University. Available online: http://www. lboro.ac.uk/research/changing.media/John%20Corner%20paper.htm.

Crafton, Donald (1993) *Before Mickey: The Animated Film, 1898–1928*. Chicago: University of Chicago Press.

Del Gaudio, Sybil (1997) 'If truth be told, can 'toons tell it? Documentary and Animation', *Film History*, 9, 2, 189–99.

Freyer, Ellen (1979) '*Chronicle of a Summer* – Ten Years After', in Lewis Jacobs (ed.) *The Documentary Tradition* (second edition). New York: W. W. Norton, 437–43.

Furniss, Maureen (1998) *Art in Motion: Animation Aesthetics*. London: John Libbey.

Grant, Barry Keith and Jeannette Sloniowski (eds) (1998) *Documenting the Documentary: Close Readings of Documentary Film and Video*. Detroit: Wayne State University Press.

Grierson, John (1979 [1926]) 'Flaherty's Poetic *Moana*', in Lewis Jacobs (ed.) *The Documentary Tradition* (second edition). New York: W. W. Norton, 25–6.

____ (1933) 'The Documentary Producer', *Cinema Quarterly*, 2, 1, 7–9.

Hall, Jeanne (1998) '"Don't You Ever Just Watch?" American Cinema Verite and *Don't Look Back*', in Barry Keith Grant and Jeannette Sloniowski (eds) *Documenting the Documentary: Close Readings of Documentary Film and Video*. Detroit: Wayne State University Press, 223–37.

Hall, Stuart (1988) 'Media Power: The Double Bind', in Alan Rosenthal (ed.) *New Challenges for Documentary*. Berkeley: University of California Press, 357–64.

Harries, Dan (2000) *Film Parody*. London: British Film Institute.

Hill, Annette (2005) *Reality TV: Audiences and Popular Factual Television*. London: Routledge.

Holmes, Su and Deborah Jermyn (eds) (2004) *Understanding Reality Television*. London: Routledge.

Jacobs, Lewis (ed.) (1979) *The Documentary Tradition* (second edition). New York:

W. W. Norton.

Keighron, Peter (1998) 'The Politics of Ridicule: Satire and Television', in Mike Wayne (ed.) *Dissident Voices: The Politics of Television and Cultural Change*. London: Pluto Press, 127–44.

Kilborn, Richard (2003) *Staging the Real: Factual TV programming in the Age of 'Big Brother'*. Manchester: Manchester University Press.

Kotlarz, Irene (1990) 'Leeds Animation Workshop', in Annette Kuhn with Susannah Radstone (eds) *The Women's Companion to International Film*. London: Virago, 240.

Kuehl, Jerry (1998 [1981]) 'Truth Claims', in Alan Rosenthal (ed.) *New Challenges for Documentary*. Berkeley: University of California Press, 103–9.

Lave, Jean and Etienne Wenger (1991) *Situated Learning: Legitimate Peripheral Participation*. Cambridge: Cambridge University Press.

McDonald, Kevin and Mark Cousins (1996) *Imagining Reality: The Faber Book of Documentary*. London: Faber and Faber.

Musser, Charles (1990) *The Emergence of Cinema: The American Screen to 1907*. Berkeley: University of California Press.

Nichols, Bill (1994) *Blurred Boundaries*. Bloomington and Indianapolis: Indiana University Press.

O'Pray, Michael (2003) *Avant-Garde Film: Forms, Themes and Passions*. London: Wallflower Press.

Perry, Emma (2001) 'In the frame: Little ups and downs', *Time Out*, 20–27 June.

Paget, Derek (1990) *True Stories? Documentary Drama on Radio, Screen and Stage*. Manchester: Manchester University Press.

____ (2002) 'Seven theses about border genres/five modest proposals about docudrama', *Screening the Past*, 14. Available online: http://www.latrobe. edu.au/screeningthepast/firstrelease/fr0902/paget/dpfr14b.htm

Pilling, Jayne (1992) *Women and Animation: A Compendium*. London: British Film Institute.

Plantinga, Carl (1998) 'Gender, Power and a Cucumber: Satirizing Masculinity in *This is Spinal Tap*', in Barry Keith Grant and Jeannette Sloniowski (eds) *Documenting the Documentary: Close Readings of Documentary Film and Video*. Detroit: Wayne State University Press, 318–32.

____ (2000) 'The Limits of Appropriation: Subjectivist Accounts of the Fiction/ Nonfiction Film Distinction', in Ib Bondebjerg (ed.) *Moving Images, Culture and the Mind*. Luton: University of Luton Press, 133–41.

Pronay, Nicholas (1989) 'John Grierson and the Documentary – 60 years on', *Historical Journal of Film, Radio and Television*, 9, 3, 227–46.

Renov, Michael (2004) 'Animation: Documentary's Imaginary Signifier', lecture delivered at University of Westminster, 6 December.

Rosenstone, Robert A. (1995) *Visions of the Past: The Challenge of Film to Our Idea of History*. Cambridge, MA: Harvard University Press.

Ruby, Jay (1988) 'The Image Mirrored: Reflexivity and the Documentary Film', in Alan Rosenthal (ed.) *New Challenges for Documentary*. Berkeley: University of California Press, 64–77.

Schneider, Steve (1994) *That's All Folks! The Art of Warner Bros. Animation*. London: Aurum Press.

Strom, Gunnar (2003) 'The Animated Documentary', *Animation Journal* 11, 46–63.

Syson, Jenny (2004) 'The Battle of Orgreave', *LeftLion*, 21 October. Available online: http://www.leftlion.co.uk/articles.cfm/id/357.

Townsend, Emru (1998) '*His Mother's Voice*: Dennis Tupicoff's New Documentary', *Animation World Magazine*, 2, 11. Available online: http://www.awn.com/mag/issue2.11/2.11pages/2.11townsendmother.html.

Vaughan, Dai (1999) *For Documentary: Twelve Essays*. Berkeley: University of California Press.

Ward, Paul (2003) 'British Animated Propaganda Cartoons of the First World War: Issues of Topicality', *Animation Journal*, 11, 64–83.

____ (2004) 'Rotoshop in context: Computer rotoscoping and animation aesthetics', *Animation Journal*, 12, 32–52.

____ (2005a) 'Distribution and trade press strategies for British Animated Propaganda Cartoons of the First World War', *Historical Journal of Film, Radio and Television*, 25, 2, 189–201.

____ (2005b) '"I was dreaming I was awake and then I woke up and found myself asleep": Dreaming, Spectacle and Reality in *Waking Life*', in Geoff King (ed.) *The Spectacle of the Real: From Hollywood to Reality TV and Beyond*. Bristol: Intellect, 161–71.

____ (forthcoming) 'Animated interactions animation aesthetics and the "interactive" documentary', in Suzanne Buchan (ed.) *Animated Worlds*. London: John Libbey.

Wayne, Mike (2003) *Marxism and Media Studies: Key Concepts and Contemporary Trends*. London: Pluto Press.

Wells, Paul (1997) 'The Beautiful Village and the True Village: A Consideration of Animation and the Documentary Aesthetic', in Paul Wells (ed.) *Art & Animation*, Profile no. 53 of *Art & Design* magazine, London: Academy Group, 40–5.

____ (1998) *Understanding Animation*. London: Routledge.

____ (2002) *Animation: Genre and Authorship*. London: Wallflower Press.

Winston, Brian (1988) 'Documentary: I Think We Are In Trouble' in Alan Rosenthal (ed.) *New Challenges for Documentary*. Berkeley: University of California Press, 21–33.

INDEX

observation(al) 4, 12–17, 43, 70, 72, 87, 95
Overall, Park 42

Paget, Derek 31, 33
Paine, Thomas 76
Pankhurst, Sylvia 76
parody 2, 12, 67–74, 76, 80, 85
participatory documentary 13, 19
Pennebaker, D. A. 14–15, 23
performance 5, 21, 31, 35–6, 41, 51, 57–8, 102
Piercy, Iain 92
Pilling, Jayne 84
Plantinga, Carl 23, 25, 28, 68, 88
Plowman, Jon 77
Power, Ryan 94
Pralle, Arlene 46
prototypicality 88

Range, Gabriel 20
reality TV 4–5, 20, 24–5, 36, 100
reconstruction 3, 7, 10, 12, 30–40, 44–5, 50–1, 59, 71, 101–2
re-enactment 10, 20, 28, 30–1, 34, 44, 50–8, 98
Reggio, Godfrey 15
Robinson, Tony 64–5
Roscoe, Jane 72, 74
Rosenstone, Robert 63
rotoscoping 91, 94, 98
Rouch, Jean 14–15
Ruttmann, Walter 15

Sabiston, Bob 91, 94
satire 67–8, 78, 81
Smart, Jean 42
Smith, Chris 72
Smith, F. Percy 83
sound/image relations 97

spectators 11–12, 21, 24, 28–30, 96
spoof 2, 24, 71, 73, 75, 81, 86
Spurlock, Morgan 101
staging 8–9
stand-up comedy 74, 78, 80
standards 24, 26, 28
Star, Susan Leigh 24
Steel, Mark 74, 76
Strom, Gunnar 88
Svankmajer, Jan 87

Thomas, Mark 78, 80
Townsend, Emru 98
Tupicoff, Dennis 98

Vaughan, Dai 30–1
Vertov, Dziga 4, 27
voiceover 3, 11–12, 35–6, 46, 62–4, 71, 75, 85–6, 90

Wachowski, Andy and Larry 25
warranting 42, 59, 63
Watkins, Peter 8–9
Watson, Karen 97
Wayne, Mike 60, 97
Webb, Tim 87, 93–4
Wells, Paul 85–9, 93
Wenger, Etienne 26, 28
Wilson, Joel 80
Winston, Brian 6, 10, 39, 50
Wiseman, Fred 14
Woolcock, Penny 35
Wuornos, Aileen 2, 21, 31, 37, 40–8
Wyatt, Ken 53

Zapruder, Abraham 7–8
Zwerin, Charlotte 8

Introduction to
Documentary Production
A Guide for Media Students

Edited by Searle Kochberg

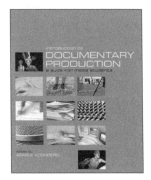

2002

192 pages

1-903364-37-X   £15.99 (pbk)

1-903364-46-9   £45.00 (hbk)

This introductory book, drawn from the industry and college experience of the contributors themselves, maps out for students the key issues that will inform their first documentary productions.

Introduction to Documentary Production: A Guide for Media Students is a comprehensive review of the main practical and ethical issues which college students must take on board in their non-fiction productions. In the book, the process of documentary filmmaking proceeds logically chapter by chapter, from research and development, through pre-production and production to post-production. Included are sections on documentary script and structure, directorial style, target audiences, production management, camera techniques, sound, editing and new technologies. The chapters are all written by specialists in their given area. Collectively, the contributors make up the staff responsible for studies in Video Production at the University of Portsmouth. For this reason they have chosen examples which help bridge the gap between the world of college and the world of commercial production.

Searle Kochberg is Course Leader of the BA in Video Production at the University of Portsmouth. He has published widely on Film Studies and acts as a consultant to various media-related organisations.

Reality TV
Realism and Revelation

Anita Biressi and Heather Nunn

2005
208 pages
1-904764-04-5   £15.99 (pbk)
1-904764-05-3   £45.00 (hbk)

Reality television has little to do with reality and everything to do with television form and content. *Reality TV: Realism and Revelation* takes the reality television phenomenon to be a significant movement within documentary and factual programming. This book analyses new and hybrid genres including observational documentaries, talk shows, game shows, docu-soaps, dramatic reconstructions, law and order programming and 24/7 formats such as *Big Brother* and *Survivor*. These programmes are both popular with audiences and heavily debated in the media; they are at the centre of heated discussions about tabloidisation, media ethics, voyeurism and the representation of the real. Through detailed case studies this book breaks new ground by linking together two major themes: the production of realism and its relationship to revelation. It addresses 'truth telling', confession and the production of knowledges about the self and its place in the world.

Anita Biressi is Senior Lecturer in Cultural and Media Studies at the University of Surrey, Roehampton. She is the author of *Crime, Fear and the Law in True Crime Stories* (2001). Heather Nunn is Senior Lecturer in Cultural Studies at the University of Surrey, Roehampton. She is the author of *Thatcher, Politics and Fantasy: The Political Culture of Gender and Nation* (2002).

'The showbiz energies of popular factual entertainment have placed an instructive pressure on our sense of what "documentary" was, is and could be. Here is a measured overview, critically astute in drawing comparisons and illuminating in the use it makes of film and television history.'
– John Corner, University of Liverpool

Big Brother International
Formats, Critics and Publics

Edited by Ernest Mathijs and Janet Jones

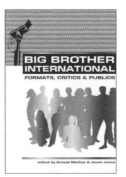

2004

288 pages

1-904764-18-5   £15.99 (pbk)

1-904764-19-3   £45.00 (hbk)

Big Brother is one of the key cultural phenomena to mark the move into the twenty-first century. Both scandal and commercial hit, it has revolutionised television practice, changing the status of live multimedia events and challenging cultural theory.

Big Brother International: Formats, Critics and Publics tells the story of its international impact. It chronicles many of the most striking moments of the show's global career, from the sexual exploits in Italy, near-bans in Germany and Africa and the cheating of Nasty Nick, to American attempts at sabotage, putting these events in perspective by linking them to their respective cultural contexts and media audiences. This multinational volume includes essays on *Big Brother* in Africa, Argentina, Australia, Belgium, Brazil, France, Germany, Italy, the Netherlands, South Africa, Turkey, the UK, Uruguay and the US. Media scholars from around the world have collaborated to compose an integrated view on *Big Brother* as a first step in our relationship with media culture in the twenty-first century.

Ernest Mathijs is Lecturer in Film Studies at the University of Wales, Aberystwyth. He is the co-editor of *Alternative Europe: Eurotrash and Exploitation Cinema Since 1945* (2004) and editor of *The Cinema of the Low Countries* (2004). Janet Jones is Lecturer in Television Studies at the University of Wales, Aberystwyth. Formerly she was an editor at the BBC. Her research has been published in *New Media and Society* and the *Journal of Media Practice*.